GALATIANS

THE TRUE GRACE GOSPEL

TRUE GRACE COMMENTARY

NEW TESTAMENT

General Editor: E Dane Rogers, MBS
Chafer Theological Seminary

Editorial Advisor: Bradley W. Maston, PhD
Scofield Biblical Institute and Theological Seminary

AVAILABLE VOLUMES:

Galatians: *The True Grace Gospel* — Michael D. Halsey

Titus: *Life in the Church* — Bradley W. Maston

*UPCOMING VOLUMES 2025–6:

Matthew: *The Chosen King* — E Dane Rogers

Mark: *The Suffering Servant* — Michael D. Halsey

Romans: *Finding the Faith* — Bradley W. Maston

Ephesians: *New Life in Christ* — Bradley W. Maston

James: *The Earliest Epistle* — Tom Eckman

Second Peter: *Holiness & Godliness* — Cody Hughes

John's Letters: *Maturing in Truth & Love* — E Dane Rogers

Jude: *Contending for the Faith* — E Dane Rogers

Revelation: *Return of the King* — Tom Eckman

*Details subject to change

GALATIANS

THE TRUE GRACE GOSPEL

A True Grace Commentary

by

Michael D. Halsey

TRUE GRACE BOOKS

Galatians: The True Grace Gospel

Copyright © 2025 by Michael D. Halsey

True Grace Books, *Tacoma, WA*

Published by True Grace Books LLC

Galatians: The True Grace Gospel / Written by Michael D. Halsey / Edited by E Dane Rogers, Bradley W. Maston / Forward by E Dane Rogers

Library of Congress Control Number: 2024903574

ISBN: 978-1-964184-44-9 (Paperback)

1. Scripture   2. Commentary   3. Bible Study   4. Bible

Cover design by E Dane Rogers

Graphics by Canva, licensed use

Printed in the United States of America

2   4   6   8   10   9   7   5   3   1

TABLE OF CONTENTS

FOREWORD

Working with Dr Michael Halsey to bring his commentary into fruition has been a singular privilege. My prayer is that this commentary will be fruitful for all who encounter it and, most of all, that it glorify God in His Son and the beauty and perfection of His true grace gospel.

Dr Halsey has a particular affinity for history. His decades of study in Scripture have uniquely prepared him for the exposition of this most important epistle of the Apostle Paul. He delicately guides the reader through some rough waters, wading through the new and unique context of the Galatian church.

With all the professionalism of a Bible scholar and the tender heart of a hometown pastor, Dr Halsey perfectly balances his prose to raise the layman up to understand the history, language, and context while providing a competitive entry to the scholarly discussions which surround the book of Galatians. It is truly a commentary for all people.

May you, the reader, find this humble volume of value, and may your study of the book of Galatians bring you ever closer to our dear Savior and the amazing grace and eternal life into which we have entered through our common faith.

Grace and peace!

E Dane Rogers,
General Editor

INTRODUCTION TO THE BOOK OF GALATIANS

GALATIANS 1:1–5

Paul wrote to the Galatians to defeat a soteriological heresy that had invaded the churches: salvation came by coming under the heavy yoke of the Mosaic law. This false teaching, if adopted, would mean the destruction of salvation by grace. Paul defends his apostleship and message as coming from the resurrected Christ; he will defend justification by faith alone; he will defend living by the power of the Holy Spirit, not the flesh. To accomplish this task, Paul, carried along by the Holy Spirit, uses a vocabulary infused with power and passion.

The epistle is encyclical, that is, Paul expected it to be circulated to other churches in the province. This practice of circulating his epistles is directed by Paul in Colossians 4:16. Paul addressed the Epistle of Galatians to several churches, not one church in the province of Galatia (Turkey), including Antioch of Pisidia, Iconium, Lystra, and Derby. Paul founded these churches on his first missionary journey recorded in Acts 13:1–14:28. He revisited them on his second and third missionary trips. The name of Galatia is derived from the 20,000 Gauls who settled in the region in 278 BC. More than two centuries later, in 25 BC, the area had become a Roman province.

GALATIANS 1:1–2

*Paul, an **apostle (not sent from men** nor*
*through the agency of man, but **through Jesus***
Christ and God the Father,** who **raised Him
from the dead) [2] *and all **the brethren** who are*
*with me, To **the churches of Galatia**.*

The Greeting

Immediately, Paul begins with a defense of his gift and calling. He does not start with words of commendation as in his other epistles.[1] This lack of any approbation for the Galatian parallels Christ's lack of commendation for the church in Laodicea, though not for the same condemnatory reason.

Verse 1

Apostle

According to *Thayer's Lexicon of the Greek New Testament*,[2] an *apostolos* is "a delegate, a messenger, one sent forth with orders." Paul wants his readers to remember that he is one of a select few backed by a divine call. This gift of apostleship carried with it special tasks such as declaring the gospel, performing miracles, establishing churches, edifying believers, and setting the form, order, and doctrine for the new body, the church.

Apostleship had a special qualification—an apostle must have seen Jesus in His resurrection body (Acts 1:21). This would mean that this gift was not given after the death of the apostle

---

[1] Cf. Eph 1:15–16; Phil 1:3–5, 8; Col 1:2–4; 1 Thess 1:2–3, 6–10; 2 Thess 1:3–4

[2] Joseph H. Thayer, *Thayer's Greek-English Lexicon of the New Testament* (Peabody, MA: Hendrickson Publishers, 2019 reprint), 68.

John, the last living apostle. Apostleship is not in existence today. Anyone claiming the gift of apostleship today is revealing himself as a false teacher.

The Church of Latter-day Saints is rife with serious false doctrines, one of which is their claim to have apostles, twelve of them. Their official doctrine states:

> Just as Jesus Christ called and sent His Apostles forth to represent Him, today's Apostles are given the role to spread the gospel of Jesus Christ throughout the world.... Jesus Christ calls Apostles to represent Him in our day just as He did in the Bible... [They are] a group of individuals who are given priesthood authority and responsibility to do God's work. The Quorum of the Twelve Apostles includes twelve everyday men with the same divine responsibility as Peter, James, John, and the other early Apostles.

Therefore, for this and a surfeit of other reasons, when their representatives knock on doors, the response should be that of 2 John 10–11.

Jesus promised His apostles a special compensation for their service, a reward described in Matthew 19:28. "Truly I say to you, that you who have followed Me, in the regeneration when the Son of Man will sit on His glorious throne, you also shall sit upon twelve thrones, judging the twelve tribes of Israel."

The Spiritual Service Gifts Today

When the Apostle John died, his gift of apostleship died with him. However, certain gifts continued. Every believer has at least one spiritual gift and the purpose of whatever the gift may be, it is to build up the body of Christ. Spiritual gifts are not a spectator sport. This would eliminate a life-long practice of believers sitting passively in the pew, observing one person exercise his gift in the pulpit. All believers are to minister to the body of Christ through their gifts (1 Cor 14:26).

3

Not from Men

False apostles who had draped themselves in the mantle of apostleship were out and about in the first century, men who were claiming the authority of Christ as given to the apostles. This fact is brought to the forefront by Christ in Revelation 2:2. "I know your deeds and your toil and perseverance, and that you cannot tolerate evil men, and you put to the test those who call themselves apostles, and they are not, and you found them *to be* false."

In Revelation 2:2, Christ uses the plural, "evil men," "those who call themselves apostles," "they are not," and "you found them to be false..." In contradistinction to Paul, these satanic counterfeits were sent from a human, not from a divine source nor through an instrument of man. This would include an appointment by a body of men or by a majority vote, or by self-declaration. Paul records that they designate themselves as apostles, but God does not.

Through Jesus Christ and God the Father

Contrasting himself with evil men, Paul uses a conjunction of contrast, *alla*, "but." Following that, the Holy Spirit directs him to write, *dia*, meaning, "on account of." His office and calling are by divine appointment from the resurrected and ascended Jesus Christ and God the Father. It was under the highest authority that Paul entered the province of Galatia to declare the only divinely certified saving message. This was not only true of Paul's entry into Galatia but also of his entire ministry as is seen from the outset in Acts 13:1–4, 44–47, and 16:7–10.

Raised from the Dead

While traveling to Damascus, the unexpected occurred; Paul saw the One whom he believed died two years earlier. It was in the dust of that road that Paul realized that he had been striving away endeavoring to stamp out the church by "ravaging the church, entering house after house, and dragging off men and women, he would put them in prison" (Acts 8:3). He suddenly understood that such efforts had been in rebellion against God who had raised Jesus the Messiah from the dead. He now realized that he had been dedicating his life to rebellion against the God of his people. Jesus was indeed alive, the Messiah!

Verse 2

The Brethren

It is not possible to know who was with Paul at this time. By referring to the brethren, he would show the Galatian churches that others agree with him concerning his gift, his divine calling, and the apostolic message of faith alone as the one requirement for salvation.

Paul not only lists himself as the sender of the letter in Galatians 1:2 but also mentions "all the brothers with me." With these words, he communicates the truth that the gospel he preaches is not merely his private opinion. All the believers with Paul acknowledge it as well, and so the Galatians are not renouncing Paul alone if they repudiate his gospel."[3]

The Churches of Galatia

These churches would be those stipulated earlier. Such recipients are unique in the Pauline corpus. Galatians is the only one of Paul's inspired letters that he addressed neither to Christians in one specific town nor to an individual.

---

[3] Thomas Schreiner, "Interpreting the Pauline Epistles," *Southern Baptist Theological Journal*, (Fall 1999: Vol. 3, No. 3), 15.

GALATIANS 1:3-5

Grace to you and peace from God our Father and the Lord Jesus Christ [4] *who gave Himself for our sins so that He might rescue us from this present evil age, according to the will of our God and Father* [5] *to whom be the glory forevermore. Amen.*

Verse 3

Grace and Peace

Paul's letter begins with a defense of his calling leading up to a doxology. He will put the word "grace" into play seven times in his letter. Grace is the linchpin of the argument of the book, that is, grace holds together the other parts of the argument of the letter.

Unfortunately, despite singing about grace and hearing sermons packed with the word Sunday after Sunday, experience shows that the simple definition of grace and its implications have been left untaught in many churches. The simplest definition is the time-tested, "unmerited, undeserved favor." By that biblical definition, the implication is that works are excluded; merits and demerits are eliminated. Grace is the basis of salvation, a base the Galatian believers were abandoning.

Paul will employ "peace" three times. From grace flows peace, peace with God. By grace through faith, the believer has been credited with the righteousness of Christ, "justified," and therefore has peace with God (Rom 5:1).

God Our Father and the Lord Jesus Christ

Paul is writing to believers by using the pronoun "our". Paul couples himself with his readers, claiming that God is his spiritual Father and theirs. The source of grace (which always precedes

6

peace in epistolary salutations) comes from both the Father and the Lord Jesus Christ.

Verse 4

Gave Himself for Our Sins

Paul points the Galatians back to the substitutionary atonement as demonstrated by the word "for." The Greek word *huper* is a word for substitution, that is, Christ died as a substitute, paying the penalty for sins. This doctrine opposes the so-called moral influence theory of the atonement. This is the idea that the voluntary death of Christ awakens love toward God; it changes attitudes toward Him and moves people to exemplify His love in their lives.

Rescued From This Present Evil Age

The gospel is a deliverance, a rescue from this evil age. Since the fall of man, the world has been dominated by evil. The apostle John pictures this domination in 1 John 5:19. "We know that we are of God, and that the whole world lies in *the power of* the evil one." John's use of "lies" (*ekeito*) is chilling, as the word pictures an infant, blissfully ignorant of the danger of his situation, lying cradled in the arms of Satan. The rescue through the atonement delivers those who trust Christ from sin's slave market as pictured by John in his Gospel (John 8:34–36).

Colossians 1:13 pictures the rescue as a transference: "For He rescued us from the domain of darkness and transferred us to the kingdom of His beloved Son." This is a rescue in the spiritual realm. Another aspect of the rescue from this present evil age is a future physical one, a transfer by death or by the rapture to be at home with the Lord, the ultimate rescue for the church.

The Will of God

The deliverance worked by Jesus Christ was not an accident of history nor was it a surprise to God. As Isaiah predicted, "But the LORD was pleased to crush Him, putting *Him* to grief" (Isa 53:10a). Jesus had known the will of the Father as early as age twelve. In Luke 2:48–49, Jesus gave evidence that He knew that Joseph was not His father. He knew that God was. He knew the will of God for His life just as He knew He was to be involved "in the things of My Father" *(tois tou Patros mou)*.

From Isaiah 50:4ff, speaking of the Messiah, one learns that God would "awaken My ear to listen as a disciple. The Lord GOD has opened My ear; And I was not disobedient; Nor did I turn back." From this morning-by-morning instruction, by age twelve, Jesus knew who He was as well as His mission to which he would not "be disobedient" and to which He would "set [His] "face like flint" to accomplish. In Hebrews 12:2, the author writes of the will of God as "the joy set before Him." In John 4:34, Jesus says, "My food is to do the will of Him who sent Me and to accomplish His work."

For the follower of Christ, setting one's face like flint to do the will of God is not floating through the years with ease. It entails living on a fallen planet in rebellion against God. The disciple has been warned by Jesus Himself: "...If they persecuted Me, they will also persecute you" (John 15:20b). Paul told Timothy, "Indeed, all who desire to live godly in Christ Jesus will be persecuted" (2 Tim 3:12). These texts show the shallowness of the health and wealth books, pious platitudes, glittering generalities, and sermons since they promise a charmed life for the taking. One false teacher claimed, "You have to permit God to prosper you...You're coming into an anointing of ease...I declare, ease is coming your way in Jesus' name."

When Paul summarized his life of faithful service, it did not include the "ease" of the pastor's declaration. Paul wrote,

> ...in far more labors, in far more imprisonments, beaten times without number, often in danger of death. Five times I received from the Jews thirty-nine lashes. Three times I was

beaten with rods, once I was stoned, three times I was shipwrecked, a night and a day I have spent in the deep. I have been on frequent journeys, in dangers from rivers, dangers from robbers, dangers from *my* countrymen, dangers from the Gentiles, dangers in the city, dangers in the wilderness, dangers on the sea, dangers among false brothers; *I have been* in labor and hardship, through many sleepless nights, in hunger and thirst, often without food, in cold and exposure. Apart from *such* external things, there is the daily pressure on me *of* concern for all the churches" (2 Cor 11:23–28).

The world, the flesh, and the devil bring disease to the godly believer.

Verse 5

The Glory

The glory of God is the goal of grace. But a serious problem had developed in the Galatian churches: God was being robbed of his glory by a teaching that destroyed the grace of God. It was the poison of works, self-effort being necessary for a righteous standing before God—legalism!

When the poison of works for salvation attacks grace, it, as the venom of a snake, works its destruction. Neurotoxic venom tends to act quickly, attacking the nervous system and stopping nerve signals from getting through to the muscles. This means paralysis, starting at the head and moving down the body until, if untreated, the diaphragm is paralyzed, and the patient cannot breathe. Around the area of the bite, necrosis can set in. That happens when the venom destroys nearby muscles, tissues, and cells. In like manner, the false doctrine which had poisoned the Galatian churches was destroying grace.

Amen

Paul finishes his doxology with an "amen." The Greek word has its roots in Hebrew. A Jewish author writes,

> The word amen is versatile and is used to respond to blessings and prayers in praise of G-d, as well as after hearing a request or supplication to G-d. When saying 'Amen' after hearing G-d's praise, one's intention would be 'the blessing that was recited is true and I believe in it,' because the word amen signifies an affirmation of belief.[4]

The meanings of "trustworthy," and "rely on it" would communicate the meaning. In the vernacular, it might be paraphrased as, "Preach it!"

Paul has concluded his greeting. He will move to the venom in the Galatian bloodstream.

During Paul's absence from the Galatian churches, a toxin got into their spiritual bloodstream. The Galatians are totally and dangerously unaware of its lethality; there are no visible fang marks nor are tissues swelling. But as the poison does its work, it will destroy the gospel Paul had preached to them, kill their joy, snuff out their assurance, damage their friendship with Paul, their spiritual father, cause the collapse of their fellowship with God, and contort them into insufferable fruit inspectors. With so much at stake, Paul confronts them head-on with a literary masterpiece as his quill becomes the hammer and tongs of truth.

---

[4] Chabad.org, "What Does 'Amen' Mean and Where Does the Term Come From?" Accessed March 4, 2025. https://shorturl.at/KYuwp

THE GOSPEL

GALATIANS 1:6–10

GALATIANS 1:6–7

*I am **amazed** that you are so quickly **deserting Him who called you** by the grace of Christ, for a **different gospel**;* [6] *which is really not another; only there are **some who are disturbing you** and [who] want to distort the gospel of Christ.*

Verses 6

Amazed

Paul "is marveling" (*thaumazo*, present tense) at the rapidity with which the venom has taken effect. He had delivered the saving message to them, a message they believed, and he had established them in churches on his first missionary journey in AD 46–47. He wrote the Epistle to the Galatians before or in AD 49.[5]

The best evidence points to Paul, having written Galatians before the Jerusalem Council, held in AD 49 and after he and Barnabas had evangelized Asia Minor on their first missionary journey (Acts 13–14). This is assuming the South Galatia destination and early date of the epistle. If this assumption is correct, it had been only a few months since his readers had accepted the genuine gospel that Paul had preached to them and had turned from it to another "gospel."

Deserting Him Who Called You

He defines the ultimate results of the poison; it is causing these believers, his "brothers" in Christ, his "children," (Gal 4:19, 28, 31) to be deserting God at the very moment he's writing the letter. Whatever is going on, the reader senses, "This is serious!" Paul's point is that the believers going *AWOL* are forsaking a

---

[5]Merrill C. Tenney, *New Testament Survey*, Revised (Grand Rapids, MI: Eerdmans, 1985), 270.

person, the very person who called them by the grace of Christ (John 6:44). They are not forsaking an arid academic system of thought or a dead-end philosophy of life. It's much more serious than that.

A Different Gospel

For the first time, Paul reveals the venom: a different gospel. A deserter leaves something and in doing so must go toward something else. By Paul's use of the word "another" (*allo*) he means "another of a different kind." What is happening is that they are being deceived by a gospel of a totally different kind.

Verse 7

Some Who are Disturbing You

While Paul is writing, the "some" are doing what false teachers always do and what false teaching always does; it "agitates," it "stirs up." To tie these results into Paul's greeting, the "another gospel of a different kind" has not brought "grace and peace" into the churches; another gospel of a different kind cannot, by its DNA, bring grace and peace because a gospel based on human merit produces two soul-crushing and unanswerable questions, "How do I know if my efforts are good enough and how do I know if I've worked long enough to be compensated with salvation?"

Those Who Want to Distort

The wolves entered the churches with premeditation. What they did, did not "just happen." Their message of works has "corrupted" (*metastrepsai*) the gospel to where it has metastasized. In medical terms, this means that the venom has rapidly spread to other parts of the body unhindered by way of the blood or lymphatic vessels or membranous surfaces. To draw a spiritual analogy, the toxin has completed its vile work, the destruction of the gospel.

13

The Gospel of Christ

The Greek word "gospel" means "good news" but a gospel of works like the false apostles in Galatia are declaring is not good news at all.

Literally, Paul writes, "the gospel of the Christ," (*to euangelion tou Christou*) that is the gospel that saves a person from eternal separation from God is a specific message about a specific person, that is Jesus' being the Christ.

What the wolves in sheep's clothing have done is to corrupt the good news of Christ. "Of Christ" is a genitive of possession *(to euangeGodlion tou Christou)*. To tamper with the gospel is to pervert what belongs to Christ. No angel, no human being has a right to tamper with what belongs to the Son of God. Thus, the genitive drives home the fact that what the false apostles are doing is a serious matter indeed, a seriousness that Paul will bring to the forefront in the next sentence as he writes with an angry quill.

As Luke records, Satanic attacks will come on the message (Luke 8:12). Such attacks have contined without surcease. Cults have tampered with Christ's precious possession as can be seen in *The New World Translation,* originated and distributed by the Jehovah's Witnesses. "It is unique in one thing—it is the first intentional, systematic effort at producing a complete version of the Bible that is edited and revised for the specific purpose of agreeing with a group's doctrine."[6]

---

[6] Got Questions.com "Is the New World Translation A Valid Version of the Bible?" Accessed March 4, 2025. https://www.got questions.org/New-World-Translation.html.

GALATIANS 1:8–10

*But even if we, or **an angel from heaven**, should preach to you **a gospel contrary** to **what we have preached to you**, he is to be **accursed**! ⁹As **we have said before**, so I say again now, if any man is preaching to you a gospel contrary to what you received, he is to be accursed! ¹⁰For am I now seeking **the favor of men**, or of God? Or am I striving to please men? If I were still trying to please men, I would not be a **bond-servant** of Christ.*

Verses 8

An Angel from Heaven

Paul now uses the strongest language of the epistle. His quill is firing from both barrels. These words are a verbal cannonade. He begins with a figure of speech, hyperbole, as he refers to "an angel from heaven" preaching a different gospel than Paul. Even if Paul himself or an angel from heaven came to them with a different gospel, they were to be cursed. An unfallen angel would never come declaring a contrary gospel just as Paul never would—this is hyperbole, exaggeration for effect.

A Contrary Gospel

A gospel contrary to what Paul presented to the Galatians would be any addition to the one requirement for salvation—faith alone in Christ alone. Such additions might be getting baptized, joining a church, performing a ceremony, feeling sorry for your sins, asking Jesus into your heart, praying the sinner's prayer (try to find one in the Bible), giving your life to Christ, committing your life to Christ, turning from your sins (try it, it's impossible), changing your geographical location (walking an aisle which has to be in a church while people are singing six verses of "Just As I Am"), asking God to save you, or raising your hand.

15

What We Have Preached to You

Luke records Paul's entry into Galatia and the gospel they received from him in Acts 13:14–41. As was his practice of "to the Jew first and also to the Greek" (Romans 1:16), Paul and Barnabas entered the synagogue at Pisidian Antioch, "and on the Sabbath day, they went into the synagogue and sat down" (Acts 13:14).

The ruler of the synagogue invited Paul to speak, saying, "If you have any word of exhortation for the people, say it" (Acts 13:15). Thus, the door was wide open for the giving of the gospel. Paul walked through that door.

He begins by tracing the history of their nation. When he comes to King David, he turns to the promise God gave him about the coming of the Savior from his descendants. It is at that point, in Acts 13:23, Paul makes the dramatic announcement, "God has brought (*egagen*, aorist tense, accomplished fact) to Israel [the] Savior, Jesus!" Those eight words are soaked in adrenaline.

Having identified the Savior, the bold and confident apostle informs the congregation of the Savior's death (Acts 13:28) and His burial which is the evidence of His death (Acts 13:29). Then Paul declares, "But God raised Him from the dead!" (Acts 13:30, 33, 37). He points them to the fact that all of this, His death, His burial, and His resurrection were all predicted in the Scriptures. He explains the reason for the Savior's death: "that through Him forgiveness of sins is proclaimed to you." (Acts 13:38).

In his message, he declares that Jesus is deity, that is, the Son of God, God's Holy One (Acts 13:33, 35). At that point, he has given them the complete content of the gospel as he states in 1 Corinthians 15:1-4.

He reaches the climax as he says, "[A]nd through Him everyone who *believes* is freed from all things from which you could not be freed through the Law of Moses" (Acts 13:39, emphasis added), i.e., works. The reader will note there are no *ands* or *buts* after "believe".

There it is. "The gospel we had preached to you"—the content of the gospel—Christ the Son of God died for your sins and rose from the dead, with its one requirement—faith—relying upon, believing, or trusting Him alone for eternal life. This is the gospel the Galatians heard from Paul, a God-appointed, God-sent apostle.

Accursed

"Accursed" is a literal rendering of the Greek (*anathema esto*). It's not a specific word and could refer to a curse in the present time, or in eternity or both. The words, "condemned," "eternally" or "hell" are not in the Greek text.

"Is this ambiguous word speaking of a believer who presents a gospel of another kind? Or is this such a serious sin that no born-again person could possibly commit after his conversion?

There is much evidence in Paul's writings that some born again believers can preach false theology and even a false gospel.

Looking at this from a practical standpoint, how would a Galatian Christian let someone be eternally condemned or let them be condemned to hell? Would this mean that they weren't to witness to them? Or would it mean the opposite— that they were to treat them as someone who is lost and personally get the gospel to them?

The solution is to let the Bible say what it's saying: the word is vague. Therefore, treat these people as those who are cursed, which would mean: Do not support their ministry financially, prayerfully, or with your time and talents. People who are proclaiming a false gospel, which in Galatians is any gospel other than justification by faith alone (Gal 2:15–16), whether they are Christians who have fallen or unbelievers who never knew the truth, are the ones we are not to aid in any way.[7]

Verse 9

As We Have Said Before

When Paul repeats his dramatic warning, he refers to what he had told the Galatians when he was with them rather than to what he had just said in verse 8. The word "said" is a compound and therefore an intensive word, "We had said plainly before" (*proeirekamen*). The Galatians had been warned in no uncertain terms, with crystal clear words from the start about those who would corrupt the gospel. Therefore, those who are deserting are without excuse.

In Acts 20:29, Paul warned the Ephesian elders about false teachers, saying, "I know that after my departure savage wolves will come in among you, not sparing the flock." They invaded the Jerusalem church, then the Galatian churches, and then the Ephesian churches. Wolves were tracking the great apostle, wreaking heretical havoc. It is no wonder that Paul listed as one of his hardships, "Apart from *such* external things, there is the daily pressure on me *of* concern for all the churches" (2 Corinthians 11:28).

The reader can feel Paul's passion for the gospel saturating the scroll as he writes the one hundred words of Galatians 1:6–9. This same fervor for the gospel message is sorely needed today.

In a men's Bible study, the teacher began to emphasize the accurate gospel message as Paul preached to the Galatians. After a few sessions with the men (who represented different churches), he asked them to relate what their pastors said during the invitation time at the close of the service.

---

[7]Robert Wilkin, "A Free Grace Perspective of Bible Translations," JOTGES, 17:32 (Spring 2004), 3.

None of them could say that they knew. This gives evidence to many a church member's indifferences to what Paul says is of first importance, the gospel (1 Cor 15:3). This malaise brought forth an assignment in a one-word command for the next meeting: "Listen!"

Verse 10

The Favor of Men

The vicious wolves sought to destroy Paul's claim to be an apostle, and thus destroy his message, by attacking his character using any means possible. Their attack was that Paul was two-faced: he preached one thing to the Jews and another to the Gentiles. In this way, he could gain more conversions by telling their itching ears what they wanted to hear.

Their charge: Paul told the Jews to keep the Law. He told the Gentiles to set the Law aside. From outward appearances, this would be easy for the false teachers to use to manipulate the Galatians. For example, Paul always used the Law lawfully (1 Tim 1:8) without putting himself under it.

For example, in Acts 18, Paul takes a Jewish vow. He could do so without compromising his message because: "The believer in the Messiah is free from the law of Moses. This means that he is free from the necessity of keeping any commandment of that system. But on the other hand, he is also free to keep parts of the law of Moses if he so desires, so long as it does not contradict the law of the Christ nor does he think that by doing so, he is gaining a right standing before God.

A modern example would be a believer's attendance at a Day of Atonement observance in a synagogue. Upon entering the auditorium, an usher will hand him a *yarmulke*. The Christian observer will not wear it to receive a right standing before God and thereby think that his name would be entered in God's Book of Life for the next year as the Jewish congregation would. He would wear it out of courtesy. (The Jew looks upon that day as the last day to get his name entered or kept in God's Book of Life for the coming year.)

Another example would be if a believer read the dietary laws in the Torah and concluded that such a diet would be heart-healthy but in adopting that regimen he knows he's not earning salvific merits.

Lawful uses of the Mosaic law would be to show the holiness of God; to show the sinfulness of man; to show the existence of absolute truth; to use the requirements of the Passover lamb to say, "Christ our Passover also has been sacrificed" (1 Cor 5:7). Thus, to use the types found in the Law's sacrificial directions would be using the Law lawfully.

Bondservant

A bondservant (*doulos*) was used to describe a person who is devoted to another to the disregard of their own interests. In the New Testament, it describes the volunary rellationship of the believer to Christ.

Saul, the up-and-coming firebrand of a Pharisee, before kneeling on the way to Damascus, never thought he would be characterized by an attitude of subservience and respect to Jesus of Nazareth or that his body would become a living sacrifice to the Carpenter.

Before the "Damascus Dusting," Saul would never have believed that he would write: "But I am hard-pressed from both *directions*, having the desire to depart and be with Christ, for *that* is very much better" (Phil 1:23). He would never say of himself, "But even if I am being poured out as a drink offering upon the sacrifice and service of your faith, I rejoice and share my joy with you all" (Phil 2:17).

When holding the cloaks of Stephen's executioners and cheering them on, Saul would have scoffed at anyone who would have told him, "One day, you are going to write "…with all boldness, Christ will even now, as always, be exalted in my body, whether by life or by death" (Phil 1:20b).

20

The man who was "breathing threats and murder against the disciples of the Lord, [the man who] went to the high priest and asked for letters from him to the synagogues at Damascus, so that if he found any belonging to the Way, both men and women, he might bring them bound to Jerusalem" (Acts 9:1–2), that rabid enemy of the Nazarene believed, knelt, and changed the world. A bondservant indeed!

PAUL'S AUTOBIOGRAPHICAL DEFENSE OF THE GOSPEL

GALATIANS 1:11–2:21

GALATIANS 1:11–14

*For I would have you know, brethren, that the gospel which was **preached** by me is **not according to man**. ¹²For I neither received it from man, **nor was I taught it**, but I received it **through a revelation of Jesus Christ**. ¹³For you have heard of **my former manner of life in Judaism**, how I used to persecute the church of God beyond measure and **tried to destroy it**; ¹⁴and I was advancing in Judaism beyond many of my contemporaries among my countrymen, being more extremely zealous for **my ancestral traditions**.*

Verse 11

Preached

Paul begins an autobiographical defense of the message he preached to the Galatians. The Greek verb "preached" *(euangelidzo)* means "to bring good news."[8] The important question concerns the source of the gospel.

Just as his appointment to apostleship was not by any man or any group of men, so his message was not from any human source. There is a "gospel" from a human source—which cannot rightly be called "good news"—in invitations to salvation which plead with the unbeliever to "feel sorry for his sins," "turn from his sins," or "confess his sins." Paul does not include those requirements in 1 Corinthians 15:1–4, nor are they found in the Gospel of John, a book written to convince the reader how he can have eternal life (John 20:30–31).

Such a requirement that a person must feel sorry for his sins is "according to men" and has been passed down from pulpit to

---

[8] Thayer's Lexicon of the Greek New Testament, 266.

pulpit, diffusing into pew after pew to the point of being chiseled into the brain where it becomes almost impossible to dislodge.

This feel-a-certain-way-for-salvation springs from a faulty understanding of "repent," which means, "change your mind" which is what the unbeliever does when he trusts Christ alone for eternal life. "Repent" is a synonym for "having faith," "believe."

Search high, search low, and you will not find "repent" in the epistle of Galatians; Paul uses its synonym, "faith." A person comes to faith in Christ for eternal life because he has "changed his mind." He has changed his mind concerning the Person (He is the Son of God) and the finished work of Christ (He paid for our sins and rose from the dead).

People have a difficult time with salvation by grace through faith alone. As one principal of a Christian school said when told by a teacher that salvation is by faith in Christ plus zero, he replied, "Yes, but there has to be more." "More" is not found in John 3:16. The "more" anyone adds is always works which negates grace.

Verse 12

Nor Was I Taught It

Thayer describes the word "taught" (*didasko*) in the passive voice as "holding discourse with others to be instructed by them."[9] The method of teaching in the ancient world was to approach a philosopher and ask him if he would accept you as his student, and for the privilege, he would be paid. The Jewish rabbis had their own students as well, a fact which Paul mentions concerning his pharisaic education under his famous teacher, Gamaliel (Acts 22:3). No rabbi taught Paul the theology of grace.

Perhaps the gospel Paul preached to the Galatians sprang full-blown from Paul's imagination like Aphrodite arising from

---

[9] Thayer, 144.

the sea. John R. W. Stott puts the question this way: "Was the gospel [Paul preached] the product of his own fertile brain? Did he make it up? Or was it stale second-hand stuff with no original authority? Did he crib it from the other apostles in Jerusalem, which the Judaizers evidently maintained, as they tried to subordinate his authority to theirs?"[10]

No! Paul's instruction in soteriology came from the ultimate, in-person source: the resurrected Messiah, Jesus, was his teacher in Arabia. Paul's course of instruction lasted three years before he received his diploma. The man who had a thorough education in the pharisaic school of works had to be trained in the principles of grace and the truths of the new dispensation, the church age. He had much baggage to jettison.

One part of his education would have been to understand Genesis 15:6, that Abraham's right standing before God came apart from works. He learned that lesson well because he used the verse to prove his argument about faith alone apart from works in Romans 4:1–16. (cf. Galatians 3:6.) To bring Abraham's name into the argument with Moses as the author of that statement for faith alone would be a strong affirmation of Paul's position. Abraham and Moses were so highly regarded as to be in Israel's Hall of Fame.

Through a Revelation of Jesus Christ

"Though" indicates the channel by which Paul's message of grace came. The channel by an *apokalypseōs*, an "unveiling." Paul wrote extensively about a veiled mind and heart. In Second Corinthians Paul wrote of the Jewish people: "For until this very day at the reading of the old covenant the same veil remains unlifted" (3:14); "whenever Moses is read, a veil lies over their hearts" (3:15); and "If our gospel is veiled, it is veiled to those

---

[10]John R. W. Stott, *The Message of Galatians* (BST London: Inter-Varsity Press, 1968), 30.

who are perishing" (4:3) and "Whenever [*someone*] turns to the Lord, the veil is taken away" (3:16).

Due to this veil, people memorize, recite, repetitively hear, and read John 3:16 which conditions a right standing before God on faith all by itself, yet somehow they "see" works crystal-clear in the text. In their veiled condition, they do not see faith standing alone, unaccompanied by any other requirement. Why? It's the veil. When Saul *turned to the Lord*, the veil came off. What a revolutionary and emotional moment that was! He had been reading the Bible all wrong, through the lens of works.

He had taken part in the lynching of Stephen when he guarded the men's cloaks so they could throw their rocks with all the force their arms could muster and as accurately as possible at the head of an innocent man until they killed him. He saw stone after stone hit Stephen in the chest and his head until, bloodied, he fell to his knees.

Then, He heard something he hadd never heard before, a man praying as the rocks were finding their marks, "Lord Jesus, receive my spirit" (Acts 7:59)! Then Stephen fell on his knees and cried out with a loud voice, "Lord, do not hold this sin against them" (Acts 7:60)!

What Saul did not know was that when Stephen declared that he saw "The glory of God and Jesus standing at the right hand of God" (Acts 7:55) it would not be long until Saul would be stopped dead in his tracks by the glory of Jesus, the Messiah.

As Paul states, the gospel he declared was a revelation from God. All the cults, all of the religions that have been, are, and will be, have a common source: fallen man. Christianity is the only revelation from God.

VERSES 13

My Former Manner of Life in Judaism

Paul reminds the Galatians that they knew his resume before the Damascus road revelation. They knew that during those years, there was nothing that would have given him a favorable inclination to this new phenomenon that was spreading. He reacquaints them with the fact that his life was soaked in Judaism.

He did not just check the boxes for a zealous Jew: synagogue attendance, the approved methods of washing hands before and after eating the proper food, and the proper prayer rituals in the practice of pharisaic Judaism. Saul put his heart, mind, soul, and body into Judaism, to the point of rising in its ranks and rising fast. He was the golden boy of the Pharisees. Paul could say, in all honesty, that the Judaism he practiced was real and meticulously so. There was not a Jew who was more into Judaism than the ever-practicing Saul.

Tried to Destroy It

Christ declared the intent to destroy (*eporthoun*—imperfect tense, repeated action) the church as an exercise in tilting at windmills in Matthew 16:18. It was an exercise in futility. There has been a long line, ancient and modern, of those who have tried to accomplish just such a satanically inspired delusion, all with no success. The ancient Roman persecutions were especially brutal.

The ten periods of persecution under different emperors began with Nero and ended with the Great Persecution during the reign of Diocletian (AD 284–305). This was especially fierce after Diocletian had issued an edict in 303 strictly enforcing adherence to the Imperial cult, when about 3,000–3,500 Christians were executed, as described by the historian Eusebius (*ca.* AD 262–340), Bishop of Caesarea.

Persecutions continued until the Edict of Milan, AD 313, under Constantine the Great legalized Christianity.[11]

The most powerful men in history have succumbed to the same destructive delusion that fevered the mind of the Pharisee from Tarsus.

Verse 14

Ancestral Traditions

At his conversion and training in grace, Paul would be forever separated from the traditional sources in the long history of Judaism: his teachers and his curriculum based on the sayings and writings of the revered rabbis of the past. He was accustomed to hearing his teachers quote these rabbis as authorities extensively and reverently. But no more did they bind him.

---

[11]Nigel Faithfill. "Evangelical Magazine," July/August, 2015: 18.

GALATIANS 1:15–17

*But when God, who had **set me apart even from my mother's womb** and called me **through His grace** was pleased [16]to reveal His Son in me **so that I might preach Him among the Gentiles**, I did not immediately consult with flesh and blood, [17]**nor did I go up to Jerusalem to those who were apostles before me; but I went away to Arabia**, and returned once more to Damascus.*

Verse 15

Set Apart from My Mother's Womb

Paul aligns with the prophets of old. In Jeremiah 1:5, God said this to the weeping prophet: "Before I formed you in the womb I knew you, And before you were born, I consecrated you; I have appointed you a prophet to the nations."

There was the one that Jesus called the greatest prophet of them all, John the Baptist. At the announcement of his birth in Luke 1:15, Luke records this prophetic word: "For he will be great in the sight of the Lord; and he will drink no wine or liquor, and he will be filled with the Holy Spirit while yet in his mother's womb." Samson, commenting on himself, knew, "...I have been a Nazirite to God from my mother's womb" (Judg 16:17).

Through His Grace

Paul sees the unmerited favor in God's placing him in his office and service. He explains how unworthy he was in 1 Timothy 1:15, "It is a trustworthy statement, deserving full acceptance, that Christ Jesus came into the world to save sinners, among whom I am foremost of all." (*protos*, "first in rank").

Verse 16

To Preach Him Among the Gentiles

This separation occurred at a point in time, that is, "from [his] mother's womb." Paul states the purpose of the separation: "so that (*hina*—introduces a purpose clause) I might preach Him among the Gentiles." This election was not "to salvation and life but to office and service."[12]

The amazing thing about Paul's preaching to the Gentiles in their environment is the fact that when a Jew traveled to a Gentile city, he felt he had been defiled. This is why the devout Jew, leaving a Gentile city, would shake the dust off his feet so as not to bring defilement upon his native land when he returned to Israel. Yet, the former Pharisee gladly goes to such towns and cities his entire life after his conversion. His change of geography would be proof of a Richter-scale shift in his attitude.

Verse 17

Jerusalem and Arabia

The gospel of grace he preached was a message revealed apart from any contact with Peter, James, and John. None of the apostles evangelized or instructed Paul. Jerusalem was ground zero for Christianity; Paul did not return to that city.

After his salvation, he went to the Roman province of Arabia which is not modern-day Arabia. The great distance between Jerusalem and the Roman province is another of the building blocks in the rock-solid edifice that the revelation to Paul of grace came directly from Christ and not from any apostle.

---

[12]C. Samuel Storms, *Chosen for Life* (Grand Rapids: Baker Book House, 1987) 148.

GALATIANS 1:18–24

*[18]Then **three years later** I went up to Jerusalem to become acquainted with Cephas, and **stayed with him fifteen days**. [19]But I did not see any other one of the apostles **except James, the Lord's brother**. [20](Now in what I am writing to you, I assure you before God that **I am not lying**.) [21]Then I went into **the regions of Syria and Cilicia**. [22]**I was still unknown by sight to the churches of Judea** which were in Christ; [23]but only they kept hearing, "The man who once **persecuted** us is now **preaching the faith** which he once tried to destroy." [24]**And they were glorifying God because of me**.*

Verse 18

Three Years Later

Paul's instruction in free grace theology was an extensive one encompassing 1,095 days. Jerome argued that that he went into Arabia to find Christ in the Old Testament. S. Lewis Johnson writes, "It was a time of withdrawal, a time of spiritual readjustment, by which he rearranged his understanding of the Scriptures under the tutelage of the Lord. In a sense, it was his apostolic training, the three years being the equivalent of the three years of training that the Twelve had had in the personal presence of the Lord."[13] Paul's experience is a necessity for a disciple of Christ, that of isolation to learn from the Lord as the psalmists instruct.[14]

---

[13] S. Lewis Johnson, "Emmaus Journal," EMJ 10:2 (Summer 2001), "Paul, His Gospel, and Thomas Jefferson *An Exposition of Galatians 1:11–24*.

[14] Psa 1:2; 4:4; 63:6; 77:6, 12; 119:25, 27; 143:5

Stayed with Him Fifteen Days

Paul did go to Jerusalem, a visit upon which the false teachers might have seized for their charge that Paul's theology was not original with him but that he was relying on the other apostles.

It is not an incidental and unimportant detail that the time frame for his visit in Jerusalem lasted only fifteen days; it would be ridiculous to think that he obtained all his knowledge in such a short time.

Verse 19

Except James, the Lord's Brother

James would be one of those mentioned in Mark 6:3 as one of Jesus' half-brothers from Mary. Jesus was not from Joseph and Mary but from Mary only. The perpetual virginity of Mary, as decreed as the Roman Catholic Church's official doctrine in AD 553, was also held by some of the early church fathers.[15] But, this decree falls apart when it collides with Mark 6:3.

Verse 20

I Am Not Lying

Paul's intensity in this parenthetical remark is significant; the false teachers were trying to damage his character. In Aristotle's *Poetics*, the ancient philosopher said that someone with a message must possess *ethos*. He wrote that *ethos* is "persuasion through character." Given the lies of the false teachers about him, Paul in this section is defending his *ethos* which concerns how reputable

---

[15] Origen, Terullian, Ahthanasius, and Jerome hold to this view as did Augustine who famously interpreted the "closed gate" through which passed the "prince" in Ezekiel 44 as a type of Mary's perpetual virginity.

33

the individual is morally in the opinion of his audience. The fact that the gospel is at stake is the reason for Paul's serious concern to defend his character.

Verse 21

The Regions of Syria and Cilicia

He left Jerusalem and went north into Syria (north Judea, by way of Caesarea) and Cilicia, the province in which his hometown, Tarsus, was located. He ministered in Syria and Cilicia for seven years (AD 37–43).

Verse 22

Still Unknown to the Churches of Judea

This is the climactic verse in this section. He is saying that he did not get his gospel from headquarters, the Jerusalem church, nor did he get it from the Judean churches. Paul did not spend time in Judea. He cites this to prove that he did not hear the gospel there where he might have heard the same gospel that he was preaching from the other apostles or from other Christians.

Those in the churches in Judea would not recognize Paul if he walked in their neighborhoods. He had not brought a sermon in their churches and there were many churches in Jerusalem and Judea since 3,000 people had been saved in Jerusalem, Judea, and from all over on the day of Pentecost.

Verse 23

Persecuted

But, oh yes, they knew about Saul turned Paul! They knew that he had been threatening them and oversaw rounding up their fellow believers—their husbands, wives, sons, and daughters, their friends, their elders, and deacons, putting them in shackles, then throwing them into the miserable ancient prisons.

Preaching the Faith

They had heard the news about what happened on that road to Damascus, the news about the man whom God would use to change the world. It was news that was too good to be true, but it was! Instead of trying to destroy the church he was establishing new ones.

Verse 24

Glorifying God Because of Me

Paul writes of the Judean churches' reaction to him and shows the difference between them and the Galatian churches that have cast aside Paul's past ministry among them. They are glorifying God because of Paul, not so in Galatia.

The Judean churches were glorifying God because Paul, once in rebellion against God and the church, is now building what he once wanted to obliterate from human history.

The Judean reaction to Paul would be a wonderful legacy for every believer. According to Paul, "There were those who glorified God because of me."

GALATIANS 2:1–3

*Then after an interval of **fourteen years** I went up again to Jerusalem with Barnabas, taking Titus along also. ² It was **because of a revelation** that **I went up**; and I submitted to them **the gospel which I preach among the Gentiles**, but I did so in private to those who were of reputation, for **fear that I might be running, or had run, in vain**. ³ But not even **Titus**, who was with me, though **he was a Greek**, was **compelled to be circumcised**.*

Verse 1

Probably Paul calculated the 14 years from his conversion date rather than from his first visit to Jerusalem (cf. 1:18). Paul visited Jerusalem at least five times, and the visit described here seems to have been his second (Acts 11:27–30) It was not his third visit to participate in the Jerusalem Council (Acts 15:1–29). This seems clear from Paul's statement that it was a private meeting (v. 2).[16]

It is important to note that this visit is not the one recorded in Acts 15, which contains Luke's minutes of the first church council meeting. That meeting in Acts 15 was not a private get-together, but an important public meeting. That meeting was to decide the question of whether gentiles were required to submit to the Jewish rite of circumcision, and hence the Mosaic law to be saved. The resounding decision of the council was an emphatic, "No!"

Since this visit is not the third visit, this would mean that when Paul wrote Galatians, the council had not yet met. Had it

---

[16] Stanley D. Toussaint, "The Chronological Problem of Galatians 2:1–10," *Bibliotheca Sacra* 120:480 (October-December 1963) 334–40.

met, Paul would have certainly used the meeting and its decision in his argument in Galatians.

Verse 2

Because of a Revelation

Acts 11:27–30 records the revelation to which Paul refers. This text contains a reference to a benevolence fund among the churches. This was in keeping with the pattern of Jesus and the disciples giving to assist the poor (John 13:29). In the New Testament epistles, there is no record of benevolence being used for assisting unbelievers.

The Gospel Preached Among the Gentiles

The Holy Spirit leads Paul to use the word *kerruso*, "I am preaching," in the present tense to indicate that the gospel he had been preaching is the same good news that he had declared when he came into Galatia. His emphasis is on the content of the gospel.

This reminds the believer to be vigilant concerning the composition of his message to see that does not present any additions to the gospel Paul gave in Galatia and stated clearly in Corinthians 15.

Fear of Running in Vain

Paul did not doubt that he had received the correct content of the gospel; he had spent three years of instruction in Arabia with the resurrected Christ as his teacher.

Instead, Paul feared that if he did not contact the Jerusalem apostles (Peter, James, and John: "those who were of reputation") the false teachers might destroy his evangelistic efforts. They could, with joy, seize on the fact that Paul had had no fellowship with the Jerusalem apostles. Wolves are always on the prowl, as the saying goes, "just looking for something."

Then, going from that assumed deficiency, they might have gone on to suggest that the reason there was no fellowship was because there was a difference of opinion between Paul and the other apostles over the gospel message. To stop this attack, Paul met with Peter, James, and John privately. They may have met in private because his relentless enemies in Jerusalem were trying to find him, and a public meeting could have been dangerous (cf. Acts 9:23–25).

Verse 3

Titus

Titus was the only gentile individual to receive a New Testament epistle. Like Timothy, he was a close associate of Paul.

Paul's respect for him as well as his familial fondness is immediately apparent. Paul referred to Titus as "My true son in a common faith;" (Titus 1:4) "My brother" (2 Cor 2:13); and "My partner, fellow worker" (2 Cor 8:23).

An important principle in the list of Paul's allies in the faith is: what Paul did, humanly speaking, he did not do without help. For example, how did Paul as an elderly, weather-beaten man, bearing the scars of service, survive his time in a dank, dark Roman prison? He had to depend on another for his food, water, and clothing, as was the custom for Roman prisoners. Second Timothy 1:16–17 supplies the answer. Paul wrote, "The Lord grant mercy to the house of Onesiphorus, for he often refreshed me and was not ashamed of my chains; but when he was in Rome, he eagerly searched for me and found me."

To tell the guards that you wanted to visit a Christian in jail was a dangerous thing to do—that is how Rome got the names of believers. Some Christians who visited other Christians in prison were executed immediately.

When Onsesiphorus left home to go to Rome he did not know if he would ever see his family again and he and they knew he was putting them in danger. That's why Paul thanked God for his

38

family's being in harmony with his trip to Rome to find and help Paul which was putting them in danger.

Even finding the place of Paul's incarceration was no cakewalk. One likes to think of the "rugged individualist," but in the service of the Lord, believers need each other. For Paul, Titus was one such "other." Paul was thankful, as one ought to be, for those God has provided as encouragers and supporters of service.

He was Greek

Titus' visit with Paul in that private session with the other apostles proved that the gospel message of Paul and the apostles were in sync. If the apostles were preaching faith in Christ plus circumcision, the apostles would have said that Titus was lost, unsaved, and an unbeliever. This proved beyond any doubt that salvation is by faith alone and that the apostles were united in that message.

Not Compelled to be Circumcised

Much was at stake in this private conference. If a gentile male wished to become a Jewish proselyte, he must submit to the surgery. To do so would put him under the Mosaic law.

In addition to that, if the apostles had compelled *ēnankasthē*, "compelled by force or by persuasion," Titus to go under the knife, the result would have been a disaster. Circumcising Titus would have split the church and the apostolic body in two, each with separate messages, and destroyed any coordination of ministry. This would also mean one group would be preaching "another gospel of a different kind."

GALATIANS 2:4–6

*But it was because of the **false brothers secretly brought in**, who had sneaked in **to spy on our liberty** which we have in Christ Jesus, in order **to bring us into bondage**. ⁵ But we **did not yield** in subjection to them for even **an hour**, so that **the truth of the gospel would remain** with you. ⁶ But from those who were of **high reputation** (what they were makes no difference to me; God shows no partiality)—well, those who were of reputation **contributed nothing to me**.*

Verse 4

False Brothers Secretly Brought In

These false brethren claimed to be believers but were not. There are warnings against these carnivorous animals pretending to be sheep in the New Testament: Jesus in Matthew 7:15, Paul in Acts 20:29, and Peter in 2 Peter 2:1. Peter adds an important note: "Many will follow [them]" (2 Pet 2:2). John agrees with Peter as to the number of their followers, as he wrote, "many deceivers have gone out into the world." (2 John 7).

The ways of false brethren will be winsome just as their father the devil wears the mask of an "angel of light" (2 Cor 11:14). A snarling wolf is not attractive; the sheep's appearance fits the bill for deception.

When the Mormons knock on your door, you will see those who come with detailed instructions regarding their sheep-like attire:

- Be neat and clean.

- Bathe, brush your teeth, wash your face, and use deodorant daily.

- Wash your hands regularly, especially before preparing food.

- Wear sunscreen.

- Wash your hair frequently.

- Choose a neat, conservative hairstyle that is easy to maintain and does not draw attention. Hair color should look natural. If you decide to color your hair, consider the time, cost, and impact on your missionary activities.

- Elders should always be clean-shaven. Sideburns should reach no lower than the middle of the ear.

- For sisters, nail polish and makeup are optional. When worn, they should be subtle in color and style.

- Your clothing should fit well (not too tight or loose); not be transparent, revealing, or distracting in any way; be clean and in good repair; be free of wrinkles; be durable, easy to care for, and suitable for your mission's climate; and be easy to pack and fit in luggage.[17]

These counterfeit Christians had entered the Jerusalem church having presented themselves as sharp-looking genuine sheep, their faces, dress, words, and manner were pleasing.

The question is, how did the wolves get in? S. Lewis Johnson comments,

> The reference to the false brethren 'secretly brought in' (v. 4), the adjective being passive in meaning, indicates that they were invited in by some of the other members of the church. Paul continues his description of them by saying, 'who had

---

[17]https://www.churchofjesuschrist.org/callings/missionary/dress-and-appearance?lang=eng

sneaked in,' a word that means something like, they wormed their way in. We have fifth columnists before us.[18]

To Spy on Our Liberty

This is a graphic and powerful metaphor uses a Greek word meaning "to make a treacherous investigation." The picture is of spies sneaking into an enemy camp, giving the impression that they are friendly, yet their purpose is lethal, in this case, fatal to grace.

Thus, the Bible uses two memorable metaphors to communicate the truth: wolves in sheep's clothing and spies sneaking into an enemy's camp. To say it another way, the Pharisees, not the barbarians, are inside the gates.

Counterfeit Christians had secretly entered the Jerusalem church and were passing themselves off as true card-carrying believers. Their message was neither Paul's message nor that of the apostles.

To Bring Us into Bondage

They intended to bring Paul and all other preachers and hearers of free grace into bondage by requiring circumcision as a condition for salvation.

Early in a pastor's ministry, two well-dressed Mormon missionaries unexpectedly visited him in his office. The spies asked the pastor for the names and addresses of the members of his church so that they might visit them and "introduce some new thinking to their minds."

The free grace pastor, realizing he was looking at wolves in sheep's clothing, applied 2 John 1:10–11 to their deceitful request:

---

[18] S. Lewis Johnson Jr. Emmaus Journal, EMJ, (Summer 2002), "The Unchanging Truth of the Gospel: An Exposition of Galatians 2:1–10."

"If anyone comes to you and does not bring this teaching, do not receive him into your house, and do not give him a greeting; for the one who gives him a greeting participates in his evil deeds." To "give someone a greeting" was an idiomatic expression that could be rendered, "Have a nice day."

Verse 5

We Did Not Yield

Paul will have more detailed instructions regarding the protocols for dealing with the wolves bearing legalism. Here he begins to discuss what he and the apostles did not do.

Using the first-person plural pronoun, "we," Paul offers more proof that he and the apostles were united in mind, doctrine, and message concerning the content and declaration of the gospel.

Regarding the gospel, there can be no negotiations or yielding as to its content. If the gospel is not conditioned on the one and only one requirement, faith alone, it is not the gospel. Period and exclamation point.

One pastor taught his congregation, "Your salvation depends eighty percent on God and twenty percent on you." The only thing he could have meant by that statement was that the members of the congregation must contribute a set percentage of work to gain heaven, thus casting themselves on a sea of uncertainty concerning when their efforts would hit that twenty percent he pulled out of thin air. In those few words, they lost their assurance.

An Hour

In constructing verse 5, Paul wanted to emphasize, "not even for an hour;" he does this by putting those words first so that the sentence begins, "To whom not even for an hour." Thus, he continues to show his passion for getting the gospel right as even his syntax demonstrates.

The Truth of the Gospel Remains

As Paul had previously stated, the Galatians did possess the gospel during his ministry there but now the wolves had come, and the churches no longer were holding to the one requirement for salvation. "So that" (*hina*) introduces a purpose clause. Paul and the other apostles had a purpose in being unyielding to the false teachers.

Paul stressed that the content of the gospel must be guarded. The guarding of the gospel was always on his mind. Nearing the end of his life, Paul charged Timothy to guard what had been entrusted to him (1 Tim 6:20; 2 Tim 1:14).

Many famous figures in American history have warned that eternal vigilance is the price of liberty. Eternal vigilance is necessary to protect the clarity of the message of eternal life. This vigilance would extend to scrutinizing those who teach the congregation from the pastor(s) to the elders to the deacons, to the Sunday school teachers. For this reason, many seminaries require the faculty to annually sign their doctrinal statement. The Galatians' vigilance was only temporary.

Verse 6

Contributed Nothing to Me

There were three results of this private conference. The first result centers on the word (*ouden*) which is "a powerful negating conjunction. It rules out, i.e., "shuts the door" objectively and leaves no exceptions."[19]

By writing, "nothing," Paul is strongly stating that one result of the private meeting was that the other apostles examined his message and gave it an A++ grade. What Paul proclaimed was complete. There was nothing any apostle could add to it.

---

[19] https://biblehub.com/greek/3762.htm

Therefore, since the message all the apostles declared was complete, one should not tamper with it by adding, "submit," "surrender," "turn from your sin," "ask Jesus into your heart," "be baptized," or "tell God you're sorry."

High Reputation

The repetition of the expression "men of high reputation" seems to indicate that it is a title given by the Jerusalem church to its leaders, which Paul uses, possibly with a tinge of irony, in depreciation of the arrogant and extravagant claims which the Judaizers were making for the Jerusalem leaders.[20]

This raises the question, "What is the content of the complete gospel on which all the apostles agreed?" Paul answers the question in 1 Corinthians 15:1–4.

---

[20] Ronald Y. K. Fung, *The Epistle to the Galatians*, (NICNT, Grand Rapids: Wm. B. Eerdmans Publishing Co., 1988), 95.

GALATIANS 2:7–10

*But on the contrary, seeing that **I had been entrusted with the gospel to the uncircumcised, just as Peter had been to the circumcised*** [8] *(for He who effectually worked for Peter in his apostleship to the circumcised **effectually worked** for me also to the Gentiles),* [9] *And recognizing the grace that had been given to me, **James and Cephas and John, who were reputed to be pillars,** gave to me and Barnabas **the right hand of fellowship,** so that we might go to the Gentiles and they to the circumcised.* [10] *They only asked us **to remember the poor**—the very thing **I also was eager to do.***

Verses 7

The Gospel to the Uncircumcised

The second result of the conference concerned a coordination of the missionary momentum of the early church. That coordination was another of the arrows in Paul's quiver launched to destroy the accusation of the false teachers that Paul was not a credible apostle.

Paul's missionary activity had a gentile focus; Peter's focus was to the Jews. If there was a disagreement, there would be no cooperation between the two.

Verse 8

Effectually Worked

This separation of missionary activity authenticated Paul's apostolic credentials to be equal to that of Peter's. As further evidence of their equality, Paul states, God was "efficiently active" (*energesas*) in both men. To use the English derivative,

46

God supplied the "energy" for both men to serve Him. Through the filling of God, the Holy Spirit, He is efficiently active in equipping the believer for service. And in such service, the believer is "blessed in what he does" (Jas 1:25).

Verses 9

Reputed Pillars

The third result of the private meeting concerned Peter, James, and John, whom Paul describes as "reputed pillars" of the church. These three recognized the right to administer the apostolic office by grace that had been given by God to Paul, that is, his spiritual gift.

Paul describes these three apostles with a word picture as being "pillars," which was used of persons "whose eminence and strength the stability and authority of any institution or organization are due."[21] This was a common term in the culture; it was in common use among the Jews as a designation for the great rabbinical teachers.

The Right Hand of Fellowship

In the Greek text "hand" is plural, "the right hands of fellowship," that is, it was unanimous. The right hand of fellowship was a common word picture in the ancient world to indicate friendship.

Instances of its usage occur both in the East and West. The Roman historian Tacitus (c. AD 56–120) uses the phrase as did other authors, stating that images of clasped right hands were sent between countries pursuing an alliance with one another.[22]

---

[21] Thayer, 591.

[22] Tacitus, *Histories*, 1.54; 2.8

It is important to note that such an act was a sign that Peter, James, and John were treating Paul as equal with them in calling, gift, and mission. By this, they were vindicating the missionary momentum of the early church to the gentiles.

Verse 10

Eager to Remember the Poor

Helping the poor was a principle inscribed in the Mosaic law, specifically to remember the poor. Leviticus 19:9–10 commanded the landowner:

> Now when you reap the harvest of your land, you shall not reap to the very corners of your field, nor shall you gather the gleanings of your harvest. Nor shall you glean your vineyard, nor shall you gather the fallen fruit of your vineyard; you shall leave them for the needy and for the stranger. I am the Lord your God.

To the observer, this would be an inefficient way to run a farm, certainly not cost effective. Jacob Milgrom comments:

> First, they were to leave the margins of their grain fields unharvested. The width of this margin appears to be up to the owner to decide.
>
> Second, they were not to pick up whatever produce fell to the ground. This would apply when a harvester grasped a bundle of stalks and cut them with the sickle, as well as when grapes fell from a cluster just cut from the vine.

Third, they were to harvest their vineyards just once, presumably taking only the ripe grapes so as to leave the later ripening ones for their poor...[23]

The believers in Jerusalem and elsewhere were sometimes in famine conditions as in Acts 11:28–30. Others were being imprisoned or persecuted. It is of note that during Paul's pre-Christian years, he was eager to wreak financial ruin to many a Christian family. Now, the very thing he wanted to "exert himself to do" (*espoudasa*) was collect money to bring aid and comfort to them.

---

[23] Jacob Milgrom, *Leviticus 1–16*, (New Haven: Yale University Press, 1998), 225.

GALATIANS 2:11-14

But when Cephas came to Antioch, **I opposed him to his face**, *because he stood condemned. For prior to the coming of* **certain men** *from James,* **he used to eat with the Gentiles**; *but when they came,* **he began to withdraw** *and hold himself aloof,* **fearing the party of the circumcision. The rest of the Jews joined him in hypocrisy, with the result that even Barnabas was carried away by their hypocrisy.** *14 But when I saw that* **they were not straightforward about the truth of the gospel**, *I said to Cephas in the presence of all, "If you, being a Jew, live like the Gentiles and not like the Jews,* **how is it that you compel the Gentiles to live like Jews?**

Verse 11

Paul, continuing his autobiography, tells of a dramatic, public clash he had with Peter, one of the pillars of the Jerusalem church.

Opposed Him to His Face

"To oppose" presents a graphic word picture that allows the reader "see" what took place between two titans of the faith. The Greek word *antesten*, from *anthistémi* is composed of two Greek words: *anti*, "against" and *hístēmi*, "to stand"). Paul takes the reader up close and personal into the passion of the event as the word involves "establishing one's position publicly by conspicuously holding one's ground."[24] At the earlier event in Jerusalem, Paul said that the apostles did not "yield in subjection to them for even an hour" (2:5). Here, there is no go-along-to-get-along with Peter when he is in serious error by his practice.

---

[24] Thayer, 308.

Implications for the doctrine of the divine inspiration of the Scriptures are found in this text. This doctrine means that the authors were "men moved by the Holy Spirit [who] spoke from God." The doctrine means "All Scripture is God-breathed" (2 Tim 3:16). Therefore, the Bible is infallible and inerrant.

But that doctrine does not mean that the authors were inspired, inerrant, and infallible in the moment-by-moment minutes of their lives. The doctrine only extends to their being inspired, "carried along" by the Holy Spirit when they were writing the Scriptures and when they were speaking for the Lord.

Matthew 16 records a dramatic example of Peter's fallibility, a time in which he was so fallible that Jesus said to him, "Get behind Me, Satan;" Peter was taking the devil's side in trying to prevent the atonement, the very reason that the Son of God came into the world (cf. Matt 2:16, etc.).

Verse 12

Certain Men

After the private conference, Peter came to the place of Paul's ministry, the church at Antioch, a church composed of Jew and gentile believers. Upon his arrival, Peter freely fellowshipped with the gentile believers exactly what he should have done. It had not occurred to Peter to abandon this time of fellowship.

But "certain men" whom Paul does not name arrived from Jerusalem to the church in Antioch. They came as representatives of James. From what happens next, it would be logical to assume that Paul was away for some reason because he would not have tolerated "even for an hour" the theological baggage they carried with them.

Eating with the Gentiles

Paul chooses the imperfect tense for "used to," thereby showing it was Peter's repeated custom to share table fellowship

51

with the gentile believers, eating together, observing the Lord's Supper together. By Peter's action of separating, it would appear to others that he's in the process of forming a gentile church, apart from a Jewish church.

He Began to Withdraw

There was no prohibition in the Mosaic law but there was an unwritten rule that Jews do not dine with gentiles, lest they eat foods off the menu of the Mosaic law.

Fearing the Circumcision

Paul now identifies his reference to "certain men;" they are the legalists who arrived from Jerusalem. By withdrawal, he's acting contrary to the divine command in Acts 10, "Arise and eat." After three repetitions, Peter learned that the menu in the Grace Dispensation had no restrictions for the believer.

Peter's action gives another piece of evidence that the church council recorded in Acts 15 has not happened; it was in that meeting that Peter stood ramrod straight with Paul and James against the legalists, saying,

> Brethren, you know that in the early days God made a choice among you, that by my mouth the Gentiles would hear the word of the gospel and believe. And God, who knows the heart, testified to them giving them the Holy Spirit, just as He also did to us; and He made no distinction between us and them, cleansing their hearts by faith (Acts 15:7b–9).

Peter's actions in Antioch are instructive: there is no personal guarantee against failure. The vaunted apostle whose name always appears first in the listing of the names of the disciples brings disgrace upon his Lord.

Paul explains the reason for the debacle: despite Solomon's warning in Proverbs 29:25, Peter was scared. This is the same person who feared being identified by a servant girl when she pointed to him as being one of those who followed Jesus.

52

Verse 13

The Jews Joined in Hypocrisy

Peter has a following in his foolish folly. Unfortunately, the number who went along with the separation was many. The seriousness of the matter is reflected in the number.

Sin is not committed in a vacuum. Failures can cause one's behavior to be imitated with disastrous results in the lives of others. Paul emphasizes "in his hypocrisy" by placing that prepositional phrase first in the sentence.

In the sentence, Paul calls Peter, the rest of the separating Jews, and even Barnabas, hypocrites. This is Barnabas, Paul's trusted missionary teammate, of all people, refusing to eat with the gentile believers, thus showing the influence of Peter's example.

It is of interest that Peter uses the same word in 2 Peter 3:17 that Paul used of Barnabas' being "carried away" to warn the believer, "You therefore, beloved, knowing this beforehand, be on your guard so that you are not carried away by the error of unprincipled men and fall from your own steadfastness." Peter had not been true to his own principles. He knew better but fear was controlling him, not the Holy Spirit.

The word hypocrite comes from the Greek theater. It describes a stage player, who, during a play, spoke from under a mask which had multiple functions during a performance:

Masks in ancient Greek theater held immense symbolic value. They served as visual representations of the characters' inner emotions and personalities. The elaborate and often exaggerated features of the masks helped convey emotions such as joy, sorrow, anger, and surprise, making them an integral part of the storytelling process.

The use of masks in ancient Greek theater facilitated multiple roles for actors, enabling them to portray different characters, even those of the opposite gender. This versatility allowed for a more dynamic and engaging performance, breaking the limitations of a single actor embodying a single character.[25]

Peter knew better and was acting against revelation from God which he received in Acts 10, not once, but three times! He knew better from listening to his own words when was not speaking from under a mask to a house full of gentiles: "You yourselves know how unlawful it is for a man who is a Jew to associate with a foreigner or to visit him; and yet God has shown me that I should not call any man unholy or unclean. That is why I came without even raising any objection when I was sent for" (Acts 10:28–29b).

Peter did not stop there as recorded in Acts 10. After seeing evidence of the gentiles' trusting Christ, he concluded in Acts 10:47, "Surely no one can refuse the water for these to be baptized who have received the Holy Spirit *just as we did*, can he?"[26]

Verse 14

Not Straightforward about the Gospel

What Peter, the rest of the Jews, and Barnabas had done was an attack on the truth of the gospel. This was not two theologians arguing over how many angels can dance on the head of a pin. This is clear from Paul's examination of their behavior. Nor was it an argument over the nuance of a Greek verb in the imperfect tense. By their hypocritical actions, they were making a heterodox declaration: "We Jewish believers have something you Gentiles do not."

"Straightforward" (*orthopodeo*) is a picturesque depiction which means "to walk straight footed," that is, "to walk in a

---

[25] https://www.lolaapp.com/masks-in-ancient-greek-theatre/

[26] Emphasis added.

straight course." Implied in their Jewish aloofness was that the gentiles needed circumcision and the observance of the Mosaic law to be complete and thereby they would be as good as the Jews. Peter has created a first-class mess!

By this implication, Peter, the rest of the Jews, and Barnabas were putting a yoke on the gentiles that God was not. God had accepted the gentile believers on the same basis He had accepted the Jewish believers—based on faith alone with no additions. To reject the gentiles was to reject God's plan of salvation. This was very serious!

Compelling Gentiles to Live Like Jews

In public, in-his-face, before the congregation, Paul drives his point home. What Peter was doing was to force the gentiles to live like Jews, whereas Peter had been living like the gentiles. Paul puts the word "compel" in the present tense to say, "You are compelling the gentiles right now to live like Jews." That was a dramatic moment, like the lawyer who asks a "gotcha" question that silences the witness, the judge, and the entire courtroom.

The believer living in the Church Dispensation is free from the Law, free from the dietary observances. To force him to read and heed the Law's menu is slavery. Peter was forcing gentiles to live under what he had already abandoned as of Acts 10. Legalism could not help it—it is always inconsistent.

GALATIANS 2:15–21

*We are **Jews by nature** and not sinners from among the Gentiles;* [16] *nevertheless knowing that a man is **not justified by the works of the Law** but through faith in Christ Jesus, even **we have believed in Christ Jesus**, so that we may be justified by faith in Christ and not by the works of the Law; since by the works of the Law no flesh will be justified.* [17] *But if, while seeking to be justified in Christ, we ourselves have also been found sinners, **is Christ then a minister of sin? May it never be!*** [18] *For if **I rebuild what I have once destroyed**, I prove myself to be **a transgressor.*** [19] *For through the Law I **died to the Law**, so that I might **live to God.*** [20] *I have been **crucified with Christ**; and it is no longer I who live, but Christ lives in me; and the life which I now live in the flesh **I live by faith in the Son of God**, who loved me and gave Himself up for me.* [21] *I do not nullify the grace of God, for if righteousness comes through the Law, **then Christ died needlessly.***

Jews by Nature

Paul moves to defend his public correction of Peter. His first defense is to return to the earlier position of the two apostles: they were Jews by birth. They did not become Jews by being Jewish proselytes to Judaism. At birth, they were born sinners among the gentiles of the world. (cf. Eph 2:1–3). However, the same realization came to both of them— "we"—neither one of them could be justified by keeping the law of Moses.

Not Justified by Works of the Law

Paul states a key word in Christian theology, a word which is also the continental divide in historical theology, separating Roman Catholicism from Protestantism. The division is over the meaning of the one word, "justified," and this divide may be summarized by "made" or "declared." In the form of a question, the separation concerns, "Is the believer declared righteous, or is he made righteous?" Protestantism says, "declared," Catholicism says, "made."

The word picture of "justified" places a person in a courtroom. There sits the judge; there stands the guilty defendant. The guilty one is declared righteous by a judicial decree of the judge by grace through faith in Christ Jesus. Roman Catholicism views justification as coming to the guilty through works; that is, the sinner makes himself righteous by various human efforts such as sacraments, confessions, and unction, an all-encompassing system of cradle-to-the-grave burdensome endeavors.

In the 16th century, because of Luther's attacks on Roman Catholicism's doctrine of justification, the Council of Trent defended its view by officially declaring in their sixth session, "If anyone saith, that the justice received is not preserved and also ensured before God through good works; but that the said works are merely fruits and signs of justification obtained, but not a cause of the increase thereof; let him be anathema."[27] It is the statement, "not justified by works of the Law" that separates Christianity from every religion of days gone by and any religion there is or ever will be.

We Have Believed in Christ Jesus

Thus, Paul and Peter came to know the one requirement for eternal life is faith's meeting the right object, Christ Jesus. Peter had made that declaration as Luke recorded in Acts 4:12, "And there is salvation in no one else; for there is no other name under heaven that has been given among men by which we must be saved." Peter had heard Jesus proclaim the same in John 14:6, "I am the way, and the truth, and the life; no one comes to the Father but through Me."

---

[27]https://www.semperreformanda.com/the-anathemas-from-trent-on-justification-by-faith-alone/

VERSE 17

Is Christ a Minister of Sin?

Paul moves to his second defense for his rebuke of Peter. It is the dominoes-will-fall defense, and those dominoes have to do with the impeccability of Christ. Arnold Fruchtenbaum summarizes,

> Though we as Jews seek to be justified, we have found that we are justified by faith through the Messiah. In order for us to be justified we must forsake our attempts to be justified by the works of the law. Now, if forsaking the law is sin, then the Messiah is indeed a minister of sin. That is the danger to Christology. We must turn away from seeking to be justified by the law to turn in faith to the Messiah, but if the turning is sin, then the messiah becomes a minister of sin.[28]

May It Never Be!

The Galatians can see the seriousness of their error in the two Greek words scorching the parchment: *me genoito*. The Expositor's Greek Testament comments: *"me genoito* repudiates a monstrous suggestion, put forward in the form of a question, the mere statement of which is repugnant to the moral sense."[29]

The Cambridge Bible for Schools and Colleges says of this idiomatic expression,

> This formula is used by St. Paul fourteen times to express a strong denial and utter repudiation of some proposition, either put forward by himself, or suggested by an opponent. "Away with such a thought!" There is neither "God" nor

---

[28] Arnold G. Fruchtenbaum, *Faith Alone: The Condition of Our Salvation* (San Antonio, TX: Ariel Ministries, 2014), 22.

[29] https://biblehub.com/commentaries/galatians/2–17.htm.

"forbid" in the Greek, but the English phrase is an excellent idiomatic equivalent.[30]

Verse 18

Rebuild What I Have Once Destroyed

Paul is adamant that he has abandoned the Mosaic Law as the means of salvation.[31] Paul's abandonment of the Law as a control over his life was a miracle, considering his religious background. As he wrote of himself in Philippians 3:5, "as to the Law, a Pharisee." Packed into "Pharisee" is the fact that "Paul, a son of Pharisees (Acts 23:6), and a stellar student of the great Pharisee, Gamaliel (Acts 5:34; 22:3), chose to be a Pharisee himself and set himself to be the most earnest of the earnest observers of the Jewish Law… "Pharisee" for Paul was not a term of reproach, but a title of honor, a claim to "the highest degree of faithfulness and sincerity in the fulfilment [sic] of duty to God as prescribed by the divine Torah."[32] For Paul, the Pharisee of the Pharisees, to have laid down the Law would be as shocking and radical a change as Thomas Jefferson's tearing up the Declaration of Independence.

A Dangerous Action

The seriousness of Peter's refusal to eat with the gentile believers is that it is a tacit statement that there should be two churches, one for the gentiles and one for the Jews. In Acts 15:9, Peter declared, "And He made no distinction between us and them, cleansing their hearts by faith." By his actions, he was living out a conflicting principle at the dinner table.

---

[30] https://biblehub.com/commentaries/galatians/2–17.htm.

[31] Cf. Rom 10:4; 6:14; 7:1–14; Gal 3:10–13, 24–25; 4:21; 5:1, 13; 2 Cor 3:7–18

[32] Gerald F. Hawthorne, *Philippians*, (WBC, Waco: Word Books, 1983), 133–134.

VERSE 19

Dead to the Law, Alive to God

The Mosaic law was a serial killer. Paul called the Ten Commandments "The ministry of death." This is because commandments carried the death penalty. The tenth commandment, "You shall not covet," is one whose violation does not demand capital punishment because it is a thought crime.

The Law provoked one to sin, and brought conviction, condemnation, punishment, and death. Upon salvation, Paul died through the Law so, upon salvation he was now dead to the Law because the Law had no more claim on him.

He was resurrected to a new law, the law of Christ, and through that Law, he could now live unto God (Gal 6:2). An important conclusion is deduced from this: that the believer in the Church Dispensation is not lawless; he is under the jurisdiction of the law of Christ.

Verse 20

Crucified with Christ

The reader is now in the realm of positional truth, that is, his position in Christ. The manner of the believer's death was crucifixion with Christ (Rom 6:1–14). Of course, this crucifixion was not experiential but positional.

Alive by Faith in the Son of God

The new life the believer lives is a by-faith way of life. "When a person trusts Christ, God identifies him or her with Christ, not only in the present and future, but also in the past. The believer did what Christ did. When Christ died, the believer died. When Christ arose from the grave, the believer arose to the newness of life. My old self-centered life died when I died with

Christ. His Spirit-directed life began in me when I arose with Christ. Therefore, in this sense, the Christian's life is really the life of Christ."[33]

VERSE 21

Did Christ Die Needlessly?

Galatians 2:21 ends Paul's autobiographical section, which demonstrates his independence from the other apostles. In this one brilliant sentence, he clinches the argument from his personal life: if a person can keep the Law to gain a right standing with God, then the nailing of the Messiah to the cross "without any purpose" (*dorean*).[34]

Seeking to stand justified before God by works is to nullify grace, which Paul did not do. The nullification of grace is the one thing that all other religions have in common. Christianity stands alone!

---

[33] Robert L Saucy, "'Sinners' Who Are Forgiven or 'Saints' Who Sin?" *Bibliotheca Sacra* 152:608 (October-December 1995): 400–12.

[34] Cambridge *Bible for Schools and Colleges*, https://biblehub.com /commentaries/galatians/2–21.htm.

THEOLOGICAL AFFIRMATION
OF SALVATION BY GRACE

GALATIANS 3:1–29

GALATIANS 3:1–3

You foolish Galatians, *who has* ***bewitched*** *you, before whose eyes Jesus* ***Christ was publicly portrayed as crucified?*** [2] *This is the only thing I want to find out from you: did you receive the Spirit* ***by the works of the Law, or by hearing with faith?*** [3] ***Are you so foolish? Having begun by the Spirit****, are you* ***now being perfected by the flesh?***

Verse 1

You Foolish Galatians

Paul begins with an alpha privative, the Greek letter alpha, when attached to a word, negates it. This is true of English too, when someone is described as "amoral," or an "atheist." In this verse, Paul attaches the prefix to *anoétos* which negates "reasoning through" or "understanding." So, he is addressing them as "the not-reasoning-ones."

Bewitched

Something has happened to the Galatians, something both evil and injurious. Paul says that someone "has given them the evil eye" (*baskainó*, aorist tense, completed act). He pictures them as having been injured by a spell being cast upon them, meaning only witchcraft could have gotten them to think in such a stupid fashion. When it comes to defending the gospel, Paul takes off the kid gloves and pulls no punches. His language is both blunt and to the point.

Christ was Publicly Portrayed as Crucified

Paul continues to return to their personal experience: He taught them about the meritorious efficacy of the death of Christ.

The teaching of that crucial doctrine of the finished work of Christ should have protected them from the evil spell of legalism.

For over two thousand years, the protection from false teachers has been the clear, definite, and plain teaching of true doctrine for which there is no substitute. The teaching of orthodox doctrine posts a "Do Not Enter" sign at the entrance of heresy's wasteland.

The death of Christ, as Paul taught them with crystal clear clarity, was totally sufficient. And his question remains, "Are you so stupid as to think that you need to add keeping the Law to it?"

Verses 2

By the Works of the Law

Paul returns to Theology 101, basic training. With this rhetorical, think-about-it question he asks, "Did you perform the works of the Law to receive the Holy Spirit?" Theology 101 has the answer. Acts 10:44, 1 Corinthians 12:13, Romans 8:9, and Ephesians 1:13–14 combine to teach that upon trusting Christ alone, the Holy Spirit is given to the believer. The answer to Paul's question is a resounding, "NO! You did not receive the Holy Spirit because of any effort of your own. You did not earn His indwelling."

By the Hearing of Faith

The answer to the question, "…or by the hearing of faith?" is, "Yes!" The Pulpit Commentary points out the meaning of this question "as describing the doctrine or message which they heard respecting faith."[35] The Galatian believers received the Holy Spirit when they heard the grace message of faith alone. This would point today's reader to Romans 10:17, "So faith comes from hearing, and hearing by the word of Christ." As in the case of the

---

[35] https://biblehub.com/commentaries/galatians/3–2.htm.

Galatians and as in the case of all believers, faith precedes regeneration.

John 20:31 makes clear that faith precedes regeneration: "But these are written that you may believe that Jesus is the Christ, the Son of God, and that by believing you may have life in his name." John's order:

1. "...these are written..." (the miracles John records)
2. "...that you may believe..."
3. "...by believing you may have life..."

Eternal life clearly is a result of faith.

Here is food for thought,

If regeneration precedes faith, then this would make faith unnecessary since the person would already be saved. If a person is regenerated, then he is born of God, a member of God's family and a possessor of eternal life. If you are a member of God's family and a possessor of eternal life, then you are already saved. So what need is there for faith?[36]

Verse 3

Having Begun by the Spirit

Paul shows the Galatians their inconsistency in verse 3. It's a matter of logic. After a person trusts Christ alone through the illuminating work of the Spirit apart from works for eternal life (John 16), then the process of sanctification becomes the issue.

Christ, in His High Priestly prayer, said, "Sanctify them through your truth: Your word is truth," (John 17:17).

The Holy Spirit's role is to sanctify the believer, "set the believer apart" (1 Pet 1:2; 2 Thess 2:13). The Holy Spirit produces the fruits of the Spirit (Gal 5:22–23). The Holy Spirit had begun

---

[36]https://www.middletownbiblechurch.org/reformed/regenera.htm.

that process in the Galatian believers who "had run well" (Gal 5:7).

Justification is immediate upon faith; sanctification is a process begun by the Spirit after justification.

Now Being Perfected by the Flesh

By using "perfected," Paul does not mean that the believer can reach the rarified atmosphere of sinless perfection in this life (cf. 1 John 1:8; Phil 3:12). Thayer's Lexicon renders the word *epiteleó* as "complete."[37] The word has to do with maturity. The sanctifying work of the Holy Spirit brings the believer to a state of maturity, completeness.

The answer to Paul's question about becoming mature by the flesh is a matter of consistency: since the Spirit began His illuminating work to show the believer was saved by faith apart from the works of the Law, He then, logically continues His sanctifying work apart from the Law, so why do you think that you must add works of the flesh to His work? He completes the work, the works of the Law do not.

---

[37] Thayer, 244.

GALATIANS 3:4–7

*Did you **suffer** so many things **in vain**—if indeed it was in vain? ⁵ So then, does **He who provides you with the Spirit** and works **miracles among you**, do it **by the works of the Law, or by hearing with faith**? ⁶ Just as **Abraham believed God**, and it was **credited to him as righteousness**. ⁷ Therefore, recognize that it is **those who are of faith** who are **sons of Abraham**.*

Verse 4

Suffering in Vain

The Galatian believers did not escape Jesus' prediction of suffering in John 15:18 and Paul's warning in 2 Timothy 3:12. Paul's question would hit home with them since, going by what the false teachers are telling them, they are not saved unless they submit to circumcision and here, they have been suffering as believers when, according to what they are hearing, they have been lost all during that time. They only thought they were believers. So, they have been suffering for no reason.

Verse 5

He who Provides You with the Spirit

In the Upper Room Discourse, Christ promised to send the Holy Spirit to the disciples (John 14:16–17).

Paul draws from the vocabulary of the Greek theater with the word, "provides" (*epichorégeó*). The word means, "to richly provide everything needed for a Greek chorus." The prefix *epi* intensifies the word to mean, "lavishly supplied."

The Greek *chorus* is not just there to decorate the stage, or to 'comment on the action' of the play. The *chorus* is intrinsic to the action—in fact, a *chorus* always plays a particular character in the play.[38]

The Holy Spirit indwelt the Galatian believers immediately upon their salvation—they did not start trying to keep the Law to earn His presence and empowerment; God lavishly supplied Him.

Miracles Among You

When Paul stayed with the churches he established.

Therefore they spent a long time *there* speaking boldly *with reliance* upon the Lord, who was testifying to the word of His grace, granting that signs and wonders be done by their hands.

In Lystra a man was sitting whose feet were incapacitated. He had been disabled from his mother's womb and had never walked. This man was listening to Paul as he spoke. Paul looked at him intently and saw that he had faith to be made well, and he said with a loud voice, "Stand upright on your feet!" And the man leaped up and began to walk, (Acts 14:3, 8–10).

Paul demonstrated that he was a miracle-working apostle.

By Law or Faith?

God worked among them without requiring them to earn His miracle-working power. The answers to this and the other rhetorical questions should have been obvious to them, but they were too stupid to see that it was all done apart from their being circumcised or keeping any of the Ten Commandments, or any of

---

[38]https://www.andromache.org/index.php/about-greek-choruses/

the other 603 commands of the Law. They did not learn. They were not thinking.

Paul then turns from the argument from experience to the argument from Scripture in 3:6–14.

Verse 6

Abraham

Over the centuries, to say that the rabbis exalted Abraham would be an understatement. Meisinger relays some of their quotes,

> Thou therefore, O Lord, that art the God of the just, hast not appointed repentance to the just, as to Abraham, and Isaac, and Jacob, which have not sinned against thee.... Abraham was perfect in all of his actions with the Lord and pleasing through righteousness all the days of his life.... Abraham our father had performed the whole Law before it was given, as it is said... *Abraham hearkened to My voice, and kept My charge, My commandments, My statutes, and My laws.*[39]

Rabbi Levi adds this, "In the world to come Abraham sits at the gate of Gehenna, permitting none to enter who bears the seal of the covenant" and "It is plain that Abraham is viewed as the warden of paradise..."[40]

Based on these over-the-top-hosannas to Abraham, if the Jews had built a Hall of Fame, they would have erected a separate building for Abraham, giving him a special edifice from the other heroes of the faith.

---

[39]George Meisinger, https://shorturl.at/VM4tM

[40]Kohler, Kauffmann, "Abraham's Bosom." https://www.jewishen cyclopedia.com/articles/362–abraham-s-bosom.

Believed God

As Paul turns the minds of the Galatians to Genesis 15:6, questions the modern reader might consider are, "What did Abraham believe?" and "What was the content of his faith?" The preliminary answer would be that it would have been impossible for the patriarch to have believed that Jesus died for our sins and rose from the dead.

The answer to the question precedes Genesis 15:6 in the context. Abraham, living in the Dispensation of Promise, believed the promises that God would give him a son, Genesis 15:1–5.

Credited to Him as Righteousness

James Montgomery Boice wrote of Genesis 15:6,

In the middle of this chapter occurs what is perhaps the most important verse in the entire Bible: Genesis 15:6. In it, the doctrine of justification by faith is set forth for the first time. This is the first verse in the Bible explicitly to speak of (1) 'faith,' (2) 'righteousness,' and (3) 'justification'.[41]

Charles Ryrie wrote: "Trust in God's *promise* is what results in 'justification'—in any era. The promises of God (content of faith) vary, but the object of faith does not. It is always God."[42]

This succinct text presents a refutation of Lordship salvation. Genesis 15:6 presents faith as the only thing that resulted in Abraham's being legally declared (not "made") righteous. In the verse, there is no reference to surrendering, committing, or forsaking sin. Those verbs must be imported into the definition of faith.

---

[41] James M. Boice, *Genesis*, 2 vols, Ministry Resources Library series, (Grand Rapids: Zondervan Publishing House, 1982), 2:98.

[42] Charles C. Ryrie, *Dispensationalism Today*, 110–31.

In Genesis 20, five chapters after the statement of Abraham's justification, Abraham sins grievously with malice aforethought because he feared what might happen to him. He lies about his wife and by that lie, his wife winds up in a pagan harem—a sin so serious that if God does not intervene, His plan and covenants given to Abraham and his descendants will crash and burn. Abraham has not "turned from sin." It took an intervention of God to undo the mess Abraham's sin created. His deliberate act was no peccadillo.

VERSE 7

Those of Faith

Genesis 15:6 is important for the Galatians and for all believers to come during the church age. Abraham's faith alone which resulted in his justification is a pattern. Faith alone is the principle on which all believers stand. They do not stand on "faith plus" which the legalists teach Whatever is after the "plus" is not the ancient pattern.

Sons of Abraham

In this portion of the verse, Paul does not call gentile believers "spiritual Jews," rather, he is saying that gentile believers are following the pattern of Abraham regarding justification as the result of faith alone. The concept the Jews had of a "son" meant to be a follower of someone. Thayer comments, "According to the Hebrew mode of speech, *uios* with the genitive of a person is used of one who depends on another or is his follower."[43] Therefore, by following the pattern of Abraham, they are the spiritual seed of Abraham but not "spiritual Jews."

---

[43] Thayer, 636.

GALATIANS 3:8–10

*The Scripture, **foreseeing that God would justify the Gentiles by faith**, preached **the gospel** beforehand to Abraham, saying, "**All the nations will be blessed in you**." ⁹ So then those who are of faith are **blessed with Abraham**, the believer. ¹⁰ For **as many as are of the Law are under a curse**; for it is written: "Cursed is everyone who does not abide by all things written in the book of the Law, to perform them."*

Verse 8

Foreseeing Gentile Justification by Faith

The concept of justification by faith was not confined to the New Testament church age which began in Acts 2. Specifically, Moses wrote about Abraham's righteous standing before God in Genesis 15:6 writing, "Then he believed in the Lord; and He reckoned it to him as righteousness."

Paul cites Genesis 12:3 concerning the gentiles, thereby showing its authenticity when he calls the verse, "Scripture." Putting this citation with Galatians 3:8, he is saying that way, way back in Abraham's day (ca. 2,000 BC), God predicted that gentiles would be justified by faith. Amazing grace!

The Gospel

Let's face it: we just cannot help it. When we read "gospel," we read 1 Corinthians 15:3–4 into the word. We are predisposed to read the New Testament back into the Old, giving the word its technical, Church Dispensational meaning, whereas, its non-technical meaning is, "a good message"[44] The word was used this

---

[44] https://biblehub.com/strongs/greek/2098.htm.

way in Classical Greek for good news about a victory in battle. Genesis 12:3 contains good news for the gentiles as stated above, gentiles would be justified by faith!

The "good message" for Abraham was that he would have a son and because he believed that he was justified. "As for the Gentiles, because they believed in the Son—the Son of God, the Messiah—they too, are saved by faith. That is the way the Gentiles will be blessed."[45]

All Nations Will Be Blessed

Only those who trust God will enter God's blessings for believers. The Bible nowhere teaches universalism, the belief that everyone will be saved.[46]

What prompts some to adopt universalism is to overemphasize the love and compassion of God to the omission of the righteousness, holiness, and justice of God.

Origin (c. AD 185–253 was the most influential universalist in the age of the church fathers). He proposed and carried universalism to the nth degree. For Origen, punishment is always, in God's intention, remedial: God is wholly good, and His justice serves no other purpose than His good purpose of bringing all souls back to Himself.

Origen wrote,

Thus the torments of hell cannot be endless, though they may last for eons; the soul in hell remains always free to repent and be restored... Given unlimited time, God's purpose will eventually prevail, and all souls will be finally united to Him,

---

[45] Fruchtenbaum, *Faith Along*, 27.

[46] cf. Matt 25:46; Mark 9:43–44; Rev 20:11–15

never to sin again. The final restoration includes Satan and the devils.[47]

Origen was a universalist on steroids!

Verse 9

Those of Faith

"So," introduces Paul's summary concerning the experience of Abraham. It has been said, "Repetition is the first principle of all teaching." Paul would agree with that statement; "faith" occurs 21 times in the six chapters of this letter. Again, "faith" has no plus sign.

Blessed with Abraham

The great blessing the believer shares with Abraham is that of justification through faith alone. Paul will draw a graphic contrast as he continues his argument.

Verse 10

Works, Law, and Curse

Although circumcision is the flash point of contention between Paul and the false teachers, it is standing for going under the entire Law. That is why he uses the plural, "works of the Law."

The legalists were telling the people that God required them to submit to the Mosaic Law in addition to faith to have a right standing before God. Paul wants the believers to understand what

---

[47]https://www.thegospelcoalition.org/themelios/article/universalism-a-historical-survey/

it means to submit to the Law to gain justification—it means a curse!

His logic is both forceful and apparent: who wants to be under a curse? To be under the Law is to be under a curse. To prove his case, Paul unrolls the scroll to Deuteronomy 27:26. To break only one command of the 613 brings a curse upon the Law breaker; to break a single command puts a person in violation of the entire Law (Jas 2:10).

To gain the severe sense of the breakage, the Galatians who were putting themselves under the Law should understand that they must keep every single command perfectly, no exceptions. Failure to do so brings a special curse.

The Law condemns; the Law hangs its violator on a tree. The Law is "the ministry of death, in letters engraved on stones" (2 Cor 3:7). Stones are cold, lifeless, and unyielding. When Paul broke the last of the Ten Commandments, he said the Law "killed (destroyed) him" (Rom 7:10). Paul's implied question is, "Do you not realize what you're doing by going under the Law? It will put you under a curse and destroy you!" The curse of the Law means death.

GALATIANS 3:11–14

*Now that **no one is justified by the Law** before God is evident; for, "The righteous man shall live by faith." ¹²However, the Law is not of faith; on the contrary, "He who practices them shall live by them." ¹³Christ **redeemed us from the curse of the Law**, having become a curse **for us**—for it is written: "Cursed is everyone who hangs on a tree"—¹⁴in order that in Christ Jesus **the blessing of Abraham might come to the Gentiles**, so that we would receive the promise of the Spirit through faith.*

Verse 11

No One Justified by Law

"No one" includes the Hall of Famers: Moses, the one who brought down the power of Pharaoh and David, the gold standard of all the kings, to name two. Yet, to read their biographies is to read a chronicle of sins. No perfect record exists among them. Scripture records Solomon's waning years in 1 Kings 11:4–6.

> For when Solomon was old, his wives turned his heart away after other gods; and his heart was not wholly devoted to the Lord his God, as the heart of David his father had been. For Solomon went after Ashtoreth the goddess of the Sidonians and after Milcom the detestable idol of the Ammonites. Solomon did what was evil in the sight of the Lord, and did not follow the Lord fully, as David his father had done.

The rabbis said that Abraham kept the Mosaic Law before there was a Mosaic Law to keep. They believed him to be impeccable. But God replies, "No one!"

Evident

To discern the meaning of "evident" (*delos*) its opposite is useful: "that which is concealed or invisible."[48] There is no way in the English language to make it any clearer than what Paul says here. Out of the seven words, "No one is justified by the Law," six are one syllable. That's clarity!

Whether in the Old Testament or the New, no one will earn a right standing before God by the Law. Yet despite this truth, countless individuals have been convinced that they are justified before God by keeping or trying to keep the Ten Commandments or by observing the ever-popular Golden Rule.

A person will often state that God will admit him into heaven, because, as he says, "I'm a good enough person." Isaiah 64:6 describes what God thinks of man's claiming to be *good enough*, "For all of us have become like one who is unclean, And all our righteous deeds are like a filthy garment; And all of us wither like a leaf, And our iniquities, like the wind, take us away."

The Righteous Man Shall Live by Faith

As Paul quotes Habakkuk 2:4, he does so to show that the Old Testament is consistent with the message of faith alone he brought from the get-go to the Galatians.

It was this verse, written in one of the most minor of the Minor Prophets, that God used in a powerful way. It all goes back to the 16th century when an obscure monk named Martin Luther, living in a dreary little village, was assigned to teach the book of Romans in the University in Wittenberg, Germany.

Doug McIntosh describes the dramatic scene:

[Luther's] superior, Johann von Staupitz, had decided that Luther needed to try something new. He ordered him to return to the university and work on a doctor's degree in

---

[48] Thayer, 131.

theology. Luther did, graduating in 1508, and receiving an immediate appointment to the faculty as a professor of Bible at the newly formed university.

His teaching position forced him to first learn the Scriptures, which he knew only from the Latin translation. When Erasmus published his Greek Testament in 1516, Luther soon had a copy and was using it to structure his lectures to teach the book of Romans.

It was while studying Romans that he made the greatest discovery of his life, the truth that resulted in his conversion. He came to Romans 1:17, where the Apostle Paul quotes Habakkuk 2:4, "The just shall live by faith."

He meditated on these words at length. Later he reflected on what happened: 'Before those words broke upon my mind, I hated God and was angry with Him because, not content with frightening us sinners by the law and by the miseries of life, He further increased our torture by the gospel. But when by the Spirit of God I considered these words I felt born again like a new man. I entered through the open doors into the very Paradise of God.

Henceforward, I saw the beloved and holy Scriptures with other eyes. The words that I had previously detested I began from that hour to value, and to love as the sweetest and most consoling words in the Bible. In truth, this text was to me the true gate of Paradise.[49]

Martin Luther discovered Habakkuk and changed the world!

---

[49] Doug McIntosh, "Martin Luther's Text," A Cornerstone Sermon Manuscript, Texts That Changed History: The Practical Ownership of Scipture No. 5, Cornerstone Bible Church, Lilburn, GA: Jan 10, 2010, Habakkuk 2:4. dougmcintosh.org.

Verse 12

The law is one domain; faith is a separate domain. The two domains never combine. To live in the domain of faith brings blessing while putting oneself under the domain of the law brings a curse because no one has never been justified by trying to keep the law.

Verse 13

Redeemed from the Curse of the Law

Paul uses the aorist tense for "Redeemed" (*exagoradzo*), signifying a completed act. The *ex-* prefix intensifies "buy out," to mean "completely buy out at the marketplace."[50]

Christ paid the complete "buy-out price" by His vicarious death on "the tree." That's why He shouts triumphantly, not with a whimper, "It is finished!"

For Us

This text refers to the price paid only for the Jews from the curse of the Law because the gentiles were never under the law of Moses (Lev 26:46; Rom 6:4 *et al.*) The Messiah voluntarily took the curse of the law (death for its breaking) by hanging on a tree.

"The Jews did ... as a mark of ignominy hang bodies on a post or stake (not a tree) by the hands after the individual had been killed in some other way."[51]

---

[50]Strong's Concordance, #1805

[51]Howard F. Vos, *Galatians: A Call to Christian Liberty*, Everyman's Bible Commentary series (Chicago: Moody Press, 1971), 60.

The failure to keep the law was the death penalty. But His death was a substitutionary one because He was perfect as even unbelievers declared He did not deserve to die (Luke 23:4, 47; Matt 27:3–4).

Verse 14

Abraham's Blessing Comes to the Gentiles

In the context, there are two blessings, one to the gentiles, the other to the Jews. The blessing of Abraham (genitive of possession) is the blessing of gaining a right standing before God—justification.

The promise for the Jews ("we") is that they receive the promise of the Holy Spirit. In the dispensation of the Law, the Holy Spirit indwelt few Jews and if He did, the indwelling could be temporary, thus prompting David's desperate plea, "Do not take Your Holy Spirit from me" (Psa 51:11). Both blessings come through faith. The Jews could never receive the Holy Spirit by earning His presence; the Gentiles could never earn a right standing before God as a payment for good works.

GALATIANS 3:15–18

Brethren, *I speak in **terms of human relations**: even though it is only a man's covenant, yet **when it has been ratified, no one sets it aside or adds conditions to it**.* *16 Now **the promises were spoken to Abraham** and to his seed. **He does not say, "And to seeds,"** as referring to many, but **rather to one**, "And to your seed," that is, **Christ***.

*17 What I am saying is this: the **Law**, which came four hundred and thirty years later, **does not invalidate** a covenant previously ratified by God, so as to nullify the promise. 18 For if **the inheritance** is based on **law**, it is no longer based on a **promise**; but God has granted it to Abraham by means of a promise.*

Verse 15

Paul now begins to focus his theological argument on showing that legalism is a failure because God's promises take priority.

It would seem reasonable that the backstory to this text is that the false teachers were arguing that when God gave the Mosaic law to Israel, He voided the by-faith alone way of salvation.

Brethren

Again, the recipients of the epistle are believers; they are his brothers in Christ. This demonstrates that a certified Christian, even one who came to faith under Paul's ministry and was instructed by Paul, could be deceived by false teaching even to the point of disseminating it.

There is an issue in the verse: Paul did not write, "and sisters" as the translators of the NASB do, putting it in italics to show its

82

addition. Briefly, "and sisters" appears innocuous; it's merely two words. But there are important issues involved, as Wayne Grudem observes:

Did the translators make the addition to follow an agenda, political or theological?

The Bible is male dominated as seen in a massive number of Scriptures, beginning with and certainly not limited to: Gen 1:27; Psa 1:1; 7:12; 8:4; Prov 1:5; Matt 4:19; Rev 18:23; and ending in Rev 21:3. To suggest that the Bible is not male dominated is absurd.

The Greek language has a word for "sister" (*adelphe*) and "brother" (*adelphos*) as we see used in tandem in Mark 10:29. Had the Holy Spirit wanted Paul to write "brothers and sisters" He would have directed Paul to write "brothers and sisters."

Additions to the text become a serious doctrinal issue and exit the innocuous as we see in *The New International Version's* translation of James 3:1: "Not many of you should become teachers, my fellow believers." The Greek text is "brothers" (*adelphoi*), the words, "fellow believers" are additions which omit "brothers." The New Testament sanctions only men as elders and the elders are the ones who teach the church. "Fellow believers" opens a pathway in today's churches for female pastors, a position forbidden by the Pauline directive in Titus 1:6.[52]

The removal or addition of words to the divine text is fraught with danger. Wayne Grudem again comments, writing about *Today's New International Version,*

---

[52] Wayne Grudem, "The 'Gender Neutral' NIV: What is the Controversy About?" in Journal for Biblical Manhood and Womanhood JBMV 07:1, (Spring 2002): 39.

If this TNIV… should gain wide acceptance, the precedent will be established for other Bible translations to mute unpopular nuances and details of meaning for the sake of 'political correctness'.

The loss of many other doctrines unpopular in the culture will soon follow. And in every case readers of the English Bible will never know whether what they are reading is really the word of God or the translators' ideas on something that would be a little less offensive than what God actually said. As Moses warned the people of Israel, so we must hear the warning today, "You shall not add to the word that I command you, nor take from it, that you may keep the commandments of the LORD your God that I command you (Deut 4:2)."[53]

Such additions lessen the biblical impact of male-led churches.

Terms of Human Relations

There would be a question in the Jewish mind, schooled in the covenant God made with Abraham. Their problem would concern the relationship of the Mosaic law with the Abrahamic covenant.

To enable them to understand, Paul will give an illustration from everyday life. When a contract has been ratified by a signature, it's not subject to change. The original takes priority, no matter what comes after.

---

[53] Wayne Grudem, The "Gender-Neutral" NIV: What is the Controversy About?" *Journal for Biblical Manhood and Womanhood* JBMW07:1 (Spring 2002).

No Conditions after Ratification

"Human relations" would include items such as wills or contracts. A will is binding until the stipulations of the will have been fulfilled. Therefore, the by-faith way of justification as seen in the case of Abraham has not been set aside by the later arrival of the Mosaic law. The covenant was "signed" by God in Genesis 15. It was a unilateral covenant because Abraham did not participate in the "signing" (Gen 15:12). It will be in effect until, like a contract, its provisions have become a reality.

Verse 16

Promises Spoken to Abraham

John F. Walvoord writes about God's promises to Abraham,

The language of the Abrahamic covenant is plain and to the point. The original covenant is given in Gen 12:1–3, and there are three confirmations and amplifications as recorded in Gen 13:14–17; 15:1–7; and 17:1–18. Some of the promises are given to Abraham personally, some to Abraham's seed, and some to gentiles, or "all families of the earth," (Gen 12:3).[54]

He Does Not Say, "And To Seeds"

Abraham had his moments of unfaithful wavering regarding the promises of God and not only once regarding the promise of a descendant.

---

[54] John F. Walvoord, "Millennial Series: Part 12: 'The Abrahamic Covenant and Premillennialism,'" Bibliotheca Sacra 108:432 (Oct. 1951).

Evidence of his quivering was his proposal to make Eliezer, his chief servant, the heir (Gen 15). God brushed that suggestion aside.

Then there was "The Proxy Plan." That idea came from Sarah, Abraham's wife, a plan to follow the custom of the culture—if a wife proved barren, she could give one of her servants to her husband to produce an heir.

In Genesis 16, Moses imitated Adam in Genesis 3, "And Abram listened to the voice of Sarai." He listened and obeyed. The result of the plan was Ishmael.

But Rather To One

After Sarah died, Abraham had six sons through Keturah. But the elect "seed" was his son through Sarah, Isaac, who would inherit the covenant and it would be passed on to one of his sons, Jacob.

That Is Christ

Ultimately *the seed* would come, *the seed of the woman* promised in Genesis 3:15. Through Him and to Him, the Abrahamic covenant will ultimately be fulfilled completely, and literally.

Verse 17

Law Does not Invalidate

The legalists claimed that since God gave Israel the Mosaic law after the promise to Abraham of justification by faith alone, then the date of that Law showed its priority over the faith-only promise given earlier.

Paul declares the opposite: the promise made to Abraham, even the entire Abrahamic covenant, was in effect. He's saying, "Listen up; you've got it backwards." With the words, "ratified by

God," he's pointing out the truth of Genesis 15 that the covenant was made unilaterally with the unconscious Abraham.

Verse 18

Inheritance: Law or Promise?

The essential nature of the promise of justification by faith alone is completely free of works. The Israelites were not to earn a right standing before God by trying as best they could to keep the Law; justification is not a salary paid for keeping on the Mosaic law diet, tithing, and building a parapet on your house.

Throughout their history, the Jews lost sight of the truth of Gen 15:6 and made the keeping of the Law the means of justification. Timothy George comments:

> The inheritance (cf. v. 29; 4:1, 7; 5:21) refers to what God promised to Abraham and his descendants, including justification by faith, which is implicit in the general term 'blessing' (v. 14). Reception of this inheritance did not depend on obedience to the Law, but God promised to provide it nonetheless."[55]

---

[55] Timothy George, *Galatians*, New American Commentary series (Nashville: Broadman & Holman Publishers, 1994), 249.

GALATIANS 3:19–22

Why the Law then? **It was added because of transgressions**, *having been ordained* **through angels** *by the agency of* **a mediator, until the seed would come** *to whom the promise had been made.* [20] *Now* **a mediator is not for one party only;** *whereas God is only one.* [21] *Is the Law then* **contrary** *to the promises of God? May it never be! For if a* **law** *had been given which was able to impart* **life**, *then* **righteousness** *would indeed have been based on law.* [22] *But the Scripture* **has shut up everyone under sin**, *so that* **the promise** *by faith in Jesus Christ might be* **given to those who believe.**

Verse 19

Added on Account of the Violations

Paul has informed the Galatians about what the Law did not do—justify the sinner—he now moves to tell them the purpose of the Law, that is, what the Law could do.

He first points out that the Law was an addition. By "added," he proves that the Mosaic law had a starting point after the giving of the Abrahamic covenant. It was not part of the numerous times God gave the covenant to Abraham, Isaac, and Jacob. The Law was not in operation in the Dispensation of Promise. This addition of the Law in no way rendered the covenant invalid.

"Violations" carries a word picture to the effect that it is a "deliberate stepping over the line."[56] Paul is using the Law lawfully when he states one of the purposes of the Law: to define sin (cf. 1 Tim 1:8).

---

[56] Thayer, 478.

Through Angels

It may seem to the casual reader of the Scriptures that Paul pulled these words out of thin air. Paul did take these words from somewhere and, as usual, he took them from God's word, Deuteronomy 33:2. But this knowledge about angelology must have been a part of the educational process for the Jews because Stephen spoke about it in his defense before the council (Acts 7:53).

There is irony in Paul's inclusion of the Law's being ordained through angels in that he heard Stephen refer to the same Scripture at his trial and at that moment, he wanted to kill the one quoting the same text he would later use.

A Mediator

Paul continues to prove the priority of the Abrahamic covenant over the Law by showing that the giving of the Law involved mediation between God and His people. This mediatorial aspect is found in a common summary of the Law: the people's responsibility was "if you do this" and God's part was, "I will bless you" when they obeyed. The converse is also true: if they failed to "do this" then God's part was to discipline them as stated in the curses of Deuteronomy 28.

This principle of is also present in a bilateral covenant in a solemn ceremony at the foot of Mount Sinai in Exodus 24:7: "Then he [Moses] took the book of the covenant and read it as the people listened; and they said, 'All that the Lord has spoken we will do, and we will be obedient!'." What the Israelites heard were serious words at an intense ceremony.

Paul's finely tuned point is that the eternal and unconditional covenant God made with Abraham involved no mediatorial moves on the part of either one involved. William Krewson writes,

God told Abram to cut three animals in half (Gen 15:9–10). "This custom enacted a solemn promise when those involved walked between the pieces of the animals. It pictured a self-curse: If the parties did not obey the covenant's terms, their fate was to become like that of the slain animals.

In this covenant, however, Abraham did not walk between the pieces. God alone appeared as 'a smoking furnace, and a burning lamp' that passed between those pieces' (v. 17). These two symbols, like the cloud by day and fire by night in the wilderness, represent God Himself. He, and He alone, walked between the divided animals. God took upon Himself all the obligations of the covenant.[57]

Abraham did not have to say, "I will be obedient" as his responsibility in the covenant relationship. The Abrahamic covenant remained unconditional and eternal before, during, and after Abraham's lying, Jacob's conniving, and the nation's apostatizing, even to the point of Baal worship and crucifying the Son of the covenant Maker!

Until the Seed Comes

"Little Things Mean a Lot" was a popular song released in 1954. It resonated with both the American and British public because it was a sentimental song that summarized the power of love and the importance of the smallest acts of affection. The same can be said of even the littlest of God's words; they mean a lot.

"Until" is one of those little words that shows the Mosaic law had a termination point. Second Corinthians 3, Romans 10, and Hebrews 7 combine in their agreement with "until" to say that the Mosaic law was temporary. The Mosaic law ended when the Seed came. In verse 16, Paul said that the identity of the Seed was Christ.

---

[57] William Krewson, "The Root of Every Blessing: The Abrahamic Covenant," https://israelmyglory.org/article/the-root-of-every-blessing-the-abrahamic-covenant/.

Verse 20

A Mediator is Not for One Party Only

With the giving of the Law, Paul points out that it needed a go-between, one to go back and forth between the parties. The two parties were God and Israel with the Law between the two. The giving of the Law involved a mediation process.

The Law originated with God, then went to angels. From angels, it went to the leader of Israel, Moses, and from Moses to the Jews.

In this process, there were two mediators—an angel served as the mediator for God; Moses was the mediator for the people. The point Paul is driving home is that when two parties have responsibilities to perform, there must be a mediation with a mediator. This is true in every bilateral covenant.

Looking at it from the nation's point of view, the Israelites were twice removed from God because, first Moses, then an angel stood between them and God as mediators. In the case of the Law, there was this separation between the Israelite and God, yet, by faith, God is directly involved with the Israelite. Therefore, faith is superior to Law.

Verses 21

Contrary

Paul finishes his section on the results of the Mosaic law. Having just written that the purpose of the Law is to define sin, Paul uses the word, "contrary," not in the sense of contradictory to faith, but in the sense of the purposes of the Law and faith. Each has a different purpose. The Law never could, nor can it produce faith.

This is crucial to Paul's argument: the purpose of the Law was not to produce justification. This is a major point of the entire epistle, a point unrealized and/or outright rejected by uncountable numbers of people today who are counting on keeping the Ten Commandments for their justification before God.

Law, Life, and Righteousness

The purpose of the Law was not to give the Jew a right standing before God. The Law operated in a realm other than faith. To think and operate in the realm of Law for justification is a futile attempt to please God because that was never its purpose.

To do such a thing produces a wasted life. There is a cliché: trying to fit a square peg into a round hole. The square peg is the Mosaic law, the round hole is faith. The square peg has one purpose. The round hole has its purpose. They do not fit and no amount of hammering can make them mesh.

Verse 22

Everyone Shut Up Under Sin

"Confined" (*sugkleió*) is an intensive word, made so by the *su-* prefix, meaning "to shut up on all sides," or "completely shut up." In Luke 5:6, there is a word picture describing a school of fish in a net. For added emphasis, Paul places the word in the opening words of the verse.

A purpose of the Law was to enclose on all sides, completely, all in a net. Romans 3:19 is a sister text on this same theme: "Now we know that whatever the Law says, it speaks to those who are under the Law, so that every mouth may be closed, and all the world may become accountable to God."

This is one of the most verifiable statements of Scripture: everyone is a sinner. This brings about another truth: fallen man rages against his accountability before God. In Mark 12, Jesus gave the corrupt religious leaders of Israel a history lesson in a parable.

When God sent Elijah, Elisha, Nathan and seventeen major and minor prophets, then John the Baptist, the greatest prophet of them all, to hold them accountable for the management of His vineyard (Israel), they beat some and killed some in their rage.

In his letter to the Galatians, he argues that when they put themselves in the realm of the Law, they are shut up on all sides by sin, completely shut up like a school of fish trapped in a net. The fish may thrash around, fight, and work as hard as they can but none of their efforts will make a way out of the net.

The Promise Given to Those who Believe

The Law traps. Faith saves. The promise of justification by faith was always God's purpose as "that" (*hina*) introduces God's intention.

The readers notice again that the only requirement for their salvation and ours is "believe." There is no "given to those who believe and…" in the text.

GALATIANS 3:23-29

*But before faith came, **we were kept in custody under the Law, being shut up to** the faith which was later to be revealed.* [24] *Therefore **the Law has become our tutor to lead us to Christ**, so that we may be justified by faith.* [25] *But now that faith has come, we are **no longer under a tutor**. For you are **all sons** and daughters **of God through faith in Christ Jesus**.* [27] *For all of you who were **baptized into Christ** have **clothed yourselves with Christ**.* [28] *There is neither Jew nor Greek, there is neither slave nor free man, there is neither male nor female; for you are **all one in Christ Jesus**.* [29] ***And if you belong to Christ, then you are Abraham's descendants***, *heirs according to promise.*

Verse 23

Kept in Custody Under Law

Paul chooses a military word to convey an important truth about the Law: the 613 negative and positive commands mounted guard as a "sentinel" (*phroureó*)[58] over the Jews. Such a condition was like being a prisoner, kept in custody on all sides.

This verse is a statement of another purpose of the peg (the Law); to act as a guard, enclosing Israel on all sides 24 hours a day, 7 days a week, 365 days a year.

---

[58] Strong's Exhaustive Concordance, #5432.

Verse 24

The Law As Tutor

The Greek word *paidagogos* (guardian) in this text has not English equivalent. It describes the function of a trusted slave whose duty it was to oversee the son in the family. "[He] was a 'boy leader,' the man, usu. a slave... whose duty it was to conduct the boy or youth... to and from school and to superintend his conduct generally; he was not a 'teacher.'"[59]

The custom of having a "boy leader" was so common in the three cultures of Paul's day (Greek, Roman, Jewish) that his readers would have immediately understood his metaphor for the Law.

Plato (ca. 428–348 BC) was familiar with the role. He characterized the *paidagogos* as "Not those who are good for nothing else, but men who by age and experience are qualified to serve as both leaders (*hegemonas*) and custodians (*paidagogous*) of children.'"[60]

Such a slave, in fulfilling the role of a *paidagogos,* bore a heavy and important role in the boy's childhood:

As a constant companion to the child, the *paidagogos* escorted the child to and from school, carrying books or other objects, sometimes securing an education for himself in the process.

He took the child to athletic practice, oversaw his meals, made him do his homework, protected him from harm, and supervised his social engagements. Twenty-four hours a day the pedagogue accompanied the child in virtually every

---

[59] BAG, 3rd ed., 748.

[60] Richard N. Longenecker, "The Pedagogical Nature of the Law in Galatians 3:19–4:7," Journal of the Evangelical Theological Society, 25 (March 1982): 53.

activity of life. In that close association the pedagogue was responsible for the moral development of the child by disciplining him when he erred and protecting him from harmful influences."[61]

From the ancient descriptions of such a slave, under the guidance of the Holy Spirit, Paul chose a most appropriate word to describe the relationship of the Law to the Israelite.

To Lead Us to Christ

The reader will note that "to lead us" is in italics in the NASB 1995, thus being supplied by the translators. The Greek text reads, "Therefore the Law has become our guardian to Christ."

The words 'to Christ' need clarification. Some take this to mean that as the *paidagogos* brought the child to school each day, he brought him to the teacher; thus, the Law's function was to bring Israel to Christ, the Teacher.

However, this interpretation is problematic for two reasons: First, the context does not present Christ as a teacher. The preceding verses have focused on Christ as the Seed, as the One who came to take the curse for mankind, and as the Redeemer [implied in the following clause and as stated in chapter 4] but not the teacher.

Second, "to" (*eis*) with the accusative case can have the temporal meaning, "until." The point is that the Law was temporary, being operational "until" the time of Christ, until the revelation of the coming faith.[62]

---

[61] Michael J. Smith, "The Role of the Pedagogue in Galatians," Bibliotheca Sacra, 163:650 (Apr 2006).

[62] Norman H. Young, "*Paidagogos*: The Social Setting of a Pauline Metaphor," *Novum Testamentum* 29 (1987): 174.

It is best to read the sentence as, "Therefore the Law was our guardian to lead us **until** Christ." To present a balanced picture, the termination of the Law should be seen as a negative. Michael J. Smith agrees:

> Yes, it had been a yoke (Acts 15:10) but Paul is here picturing that ending as the finishing of an era of Israel's childhood relationship with God.

> The termination brought a promising future of an attractive new dispensation. Their childhood was over; a new familial relationship, a relationship of faith, the control of the Spirit and the fellowship of all believers, Jew and gentile, was about to begin.

> The Law had protected Israel just as the *paidagogos* did the child and the household. The Law had guarded Israel from the religious heathenism of the surrounding Gentiles.[63]

The Law had sealed them off to prevent them from going the way of the Amorites, the Hittites, the Perizzites, the Canaanites, the Hivites, and the Jebusites into history's boneyard.

Verses 25

No Longer Under a Guardian

Out with the old, in with the new! Dispensationally, a new day dawned on a mountain. Not Mt. Sinai but Mt. Calvary. At the proper time, the boy was no longer a child. It was at that time, his relationship to the *paidagogos* was no more.

Xenophon, a philosopher historian, a contemporary of Plato, and a student of Socrates, wrote,

---

[63] Michael J. Smith, "The Role of the Pedagogue in Galatians," BSAC 163:650 (April–June 2006), 197.

When a boy ceases to be a child, and begins to be a lad, others release him from his moral tutor (*paidagogos*) and his schoolmaster: he is then no longer under a ruler and is allowed to go his own way.[64]

Our justification by faith alone brings with it certain results. It brought with it the status of maturity. In their first year at Dallas Theological Seminary, John F. Walwood would say to the entering class who would be living in the dormitory,

We do not have a lights-out policy. We do not have a be-in-bed time. The door to the building is never locked. You decide when to come into the building, when to turn out your lights, and when to go to bed. There will be no one to monitor you coming and going. That's because we're training leaders here and leaders don't need to be told such things.

There was no punishment for studying all night. There were no demerits to the student's account. There was no staying after school. The role of the *paidagogos* was essentially harsh as Timothy George relates,

No doubt there were many pedagogues who were known for their kindness and held in affection by their wards, but the dominant image was that of a harsh disciplinarian who frequently resorted to physical force and corporal punishment as a way of keeping his children in line.[65]

There was no need for such a regimen in the dorm.

---

[64] Xenophon, *Constitution of the Lacedaemonians*, 3.1, trans. E. C. Marchant, Loeb Classical Library (London: William Heinemann, 1925).

[65] Timothy George, 265.

Verse 26

Sons of God

As stated above in Galatians 3:15, the NASB has inserted words not in the Greek of that verse.

In the sunshine of the new dispensation, the child, having left the *paidagogos* to his new status, has the new legal position with its rights and privileges. The most common age range for being legally a child in Paul's day was six to sixteen. When the Roman child became an "adult son" (*huioi*) at age seventeen he was free from the *paidagogos*. No longer was he under his authority.

Through Faith in Christ Jesus

By this statement, Paul is teaching through the pedagogical method of repetition. Richard F. Bruner comments on this important aspect of teaching:

> One of the biggest mistakes a teacher can make is to forgo the return or repetition. The learning process is one of slow engagement with ideas; gradually the engagement builds to a critical mass when the student actually acquires the idea. Repetition matters because it can hasten and deepen the engagement process. If one cares about quality of learning, one should consciously design repetitive engagement into courses and daily teaching.[66]

---

[66] Richard F. Bruner, "Repetition is the First Principle of All Learning," August 2001.

Verses 27–28

Baptized Into Christ

Upon faith in Christ, the believer is immediately moved into a new position by one of the seven baptisms mentioned in Scripture, the baptism of the Spirit. This dry baptism finds its classic text in 1 Corinthians 12:13: "For by one Spirit we were all baptized into one body, whether Jews or Greeks, whether slaves or free, and we were all made to drink of one Spirit."

Charles Ryrie defines this baptism:

The baptizing work of the Spirit is the one work of the Spirit that is not found in any other dispensation. This can be demonstrated theologically and biblically (1 Cor 12:13). ...The baptizing work of the Spirit is that which places a person in the body of Christ. Since the body of Christ.... is distinctive to this age, then so is the baptism.[67]

Clothed

With this word, Paul returns to the description of the "adult son of God." There were six different types of togas worn in the Roman Empire whose function was to denote status. Two of those types applied to the child/adult son. The youth wore the Toga Praetexta, a toga with a woven reddish-purple border. At the end of adolescence, a male put on the white *Toga Virilis*, the toga of manhood.[68]

---

[67] Charles C. Ryrie, *The Holy Spirit* (Chicago: Moody, 1965, 1997), 108–12; see also John F. Walvoord, The Holy Spirit, (Grand Rapids: Zondervan, 1954), 108.

[68] N. S. Gill, "The Six Types of Togas Worn in Ancient Rome," (Thought Co.) https://www.thoughtco.com/six-types-of-toga-in-ancient-rome-117805.

This was an important day in a young boy's life—so important that there would be accompanied by a solemn ceremony as described by Jamie Frater:

> As teenagers, Roman males would have coming-of-age ceremonies to mark that they had officially become citizens of Rome. ...usually between the ages of 14 and 17.

> For the ceremony, the boy would take off his *bulla*, a necklace that provided protection and was given to the child at birth, and offer it to the Lares (guardian deities). He also stopped wearing a toga with a crimson border, which signified childhood. Instead, he started wearing a pure white toga, just like that of a grown man.

> Then there would be a large procession to the Forum. There, the boy's name would be added to the list of citizens. Afterward, the boy and his family would go to the temple of Liber on Capitoline Hill to make an offering before they returned home for a feast.

> After this, the boy would spend a year with a man chosen by his father. The man would teach the teen how to excel in either army or civic duties.[69]

By the baptism of the Holy Spirit, the believer has put on Christ, thus completing the analogy of going from the immature age of the Law to the mature age of Grace.

All One in Christ Jesus

The reader should take care to keep the truth of "all" in context. As Paul lists Jew, gentile, male, female, etc., he is not saying that there are no distinctions among those listed. There are differences and those remain after the baptism of the Spirit.

---

[69] "10 Ancient Coming-of-Age Rituals," https://listverse.com/2019/02/22/10-ancient-coming-of-age-rituals/.

The context is faith alone as the one requirement for the baptism of the Holy Spirit. In this, "there is neither Jew nor Greek, there is neither slave nor free, there is neither male nor female." For emphasis, Paul repeats "there is" three times, thus stressing that one requirement of faith is for "all." In the area of justification, there are no distinctions.

Verse 29

Abraham's Descendants Belong to Christ

Going by the context and Paul's argument in the book, believers are called Abraham's "seed" (*sperma*), a descendent of Abraham spiritually through justification by faith alone. This does not mean that the gentile believer becomes a Jew or a spiritual Jew.

This does not mean that because of being of the seed of Abraham, the believer has become an "heir" of all of God's promises to the patriarch. God promised some things to all the physical descendants of Abraham (e.g., Gen 12:1–2, 7). He promised other things to the gentile believers (Gen 12:3).

The spiritual seed of Abraham are never called "Israel." The spiritual seed are not inheritors of the physical, national, or material promises made to the Jews in the Abrahamic covenant.

THE SONSHIP OF CHRIST

GALATIANS 4:1–20

GALATIANS 4:1-3

*Now I say, as long **as the heir is a child, he does not differ at all from a slave** although he is owner of everything,* [2] *but he is under guardians and managers until **the date set by the father**.* [3] *So also we, **while we were children**, were held in bondage under the **elementary things** of the world.*

Verse 1

When the doctrine gets hard, the human mind craves illustrations. As Paul begins chapter 4, he will now clarify the doctrine domestically (vv. 1–11), historically (vv. 12–20), and biblically (vv. 21–31). Paul begins with the familial.

In verses 1–2, Paul brings clarity with the first illustration based on domestic relationships in the ancient world.

A Child Heir Does Not Differ from a Slave

The issue is immaturity as opposed to maturity, as illustrated by a child in the family. In Jewish circles, the child was defined as someone ages 1–11; in Greece a child was defined as being 1–17 years of age; and under Roman law a child was ages 1–13.[70]

While in that legal state which defined the parameters of childhood, the boy had no more rights than a slave in the Roman Empire. He had fewer rights than a slave because of the 360-degree oversight of the *paidagogos*.

Slaves did have a modicum of rights in the Empire: "They could file complaints for severe mistreatment... Slaves were

---

[70] William Barclay, *The Letters to the Galatians and Ephesians,* The Daily Study Bible Series, 2nd ed. (Edinburgh: Saint Andrew Press, 1962), 36–37.

usually paid in the Roman world, with a *perculium*. Although this was only a very modest salary it did allow the slave some freedom to purchase certain goods…"[71]

Verse 2

The Date Set by the Father

The boy was managed and guarded within that circle. Even though he was the heir, until his father set the date for his becoming a full-fledged, registered, and legal adult, he remained a child with no authority and always under the authority of others year after year. The child had no legal right to set the date of his entrance into adulthood.

Verse 3

While We Were Children

Paul now draws the application of the domestic illustration as he refers to both Jews and gentiles, classifying both as immature. Each had their own enslavement; the Jews were under the rule of the Mosaic law while the gentiles were under the bondage of paganism with its rituals.

Rudimentary Principles

The "elementary principles" (*stoicheia*) is a picturesque word to describe the ABCs—"the letters of the alphabet as the elements

---

[71] Daniel Kershaw, "Roman Slaves: Slavery in Ancient Rome," *History Cooperative*, July 10, 2023, https://historycooperative.org/roman-slaves/

of speech, not however the written characters (which are called *grammmata*) but the spoken sounds."[72]

The bondage of the elemental principles for the gentiles in the Roman Empire would be such things as "requests and prayers presented to gods as a trade:

> if the god did what was requested, then the worshiper promised to do a particular thing in return. This trade was binding. To persuade the gods to favor the requests, a worshiper might make offerings of food or wine, or would carry out a ritual sacrifice of an animal before eating it.

> The Romans believed that their gods or spirits were actively involved in their daily lives. As a result, sacred meals were held in their name during certain religious festivals. It was believed that the god actually took part in the meal: a place was set for him at the table, invitations were issued in his name, and a portion of the food served was set aside for him to enjoy. At home, the paterfamilias—head of the family—performed religious rituals for the household.[73]

Because of what Paul says at this point, the Law was holding the Israelite in a state of perpetual immaturity. Spiritually speaking, their childhood lasted approximately 1,500 years.

---

[72] Thayer, 588–89.

[73] "The Roman Empire in the First Century: Worship," https://www.pbs.org/empires/romans/empire/worship.html.

GALATIANS 4:4–7

*But when the **fullness of the time** came, God sent forth His Son, **born of a woman**, born **under the Law**, ⁵ so that He might **redeem those who were under the Law**, that we might receive the **adoption as sons**. ⁶ Because you are sons, God has sent forth **the Spirit** of His Son into our hearts, **crying, "Abba! Father!"** ⁷ Therefore you are **no longer a slave, but a son**; and if a son, then an heir through God.*

Verse 4

Fullness of Time

When the Messiah came, that advent was at a set time, the proper time politically, spiritually, and morally. Politically, The first advent of Christ, was during the time historians call the "*Pax Romana*," Roman Peace.

Christopher Klein writes,

After decades of political dysfunction, civil wars and assassinations... Rome flourished during two centuries of relative tranquility and prosperity known as the Pax Romana. Ushered in by the ascension of Augustus as the first Roman emperor in 27 BC, this era of political stability and security lasted until the death of Marcus Aurelius in AD 180[74]

During this time, the Roman military built a magnificent interstate highway system of no fewer than 29 great military highways radiating from the capital, and the late Empire's 113 provinces were interconnected by 372 great roads. The entire

---

[74] Christopher Klein, "How Ancient Rome Thrived During Pax Romana," Aug 18, 2021, https://www.history.com/articles/pax-romana-roman-empire-peace-augustus.

system comprised more than 250,000 miles of roads, of which over 50,000 miles were stone-paved! When coupled with the aspect of stability and security brought by the Pax Romana, this allowed the gospel to travel far and wide with alacrity.

In addition, Roman law gave protection to the Roman citizen, a protection Paul, a Roman citizen, used to the benefit of his ministry. In Acts 25:11, while standing before a Roman tribunal, Paul declared his legal right, saying, "I appeal to Caesar!" Longenecker writes, "His 'appeal' for a trial in Rome before 'Caesar' was the right of every Roman citizen who believed that he was in danger of violent coercion or capital punishment in a lower court."[75]

In Philippi, when Paul was the victim of a miscarriage of justice--he was beaten in court and thrown in jail. The next day, because of Roman law, the following drama ensued:

> Now when day came, the chief magistrates sent their policemen, saying, "Release those men." And the jailer reported these words to Paul, saying, "The chief magistrates have sent to release you. Therefore come out now and go in peace." But Paul said to them, "They have beaten us in public without trial, men who are Romans, and have thrown us into prison; and now are they sending us away secretly? No indeed! But let them come themselves and bring us out." The policemen reported these words to the chief magistrates. They were afraid when they heard that they were Romans, and they came and appealed to them, and when they had brought them out, they kept begging them to leave the city (Acts 16:35–39).

During the time of the Pax Romana, a common language united the Empire, the Koine Greek. Not only was Koine Greek

---

[75] Richard N. Longenecker, "The Acts of the Apostles." In *John–Acts*. Vol. 9 of *The Expositor's Bible Commentary*, 12 vols. Ed. by Frank E. Gaebelein and J. D. Douglas (Grand Rapids: Zondervan, 1981), 545.

common in the sense it enjoyed widespread usage throughout the Roman Empire, but it was also common in the sense that it was not the language of the intellectual and academic elites. Classical Greek was used by the educated class.

> Koine Greek was the language of the working man, the peasant, the vendor, and the housewife—there was nothing pretentious about it. It was the vernacular, or vulgar language, of the day. The great works of Greek literature were written in Classical Greek. No scholar today would care to study anything written in Koine Greek, except for the fact that it is the language of the New Testament. God wanted His Word to be accessible to everyone, and He chose the common language of the day, Koine.[76]

Thus, the Koine Greek allowed the gospel and the New Testament to spread rapidly without needing groups of trained translators.

Spiritually and morally, the old and fatigued classical religions of Greece and Rome were bankrupt. Tom Holland, writing about the immorality of the Caesars beginning with Tiberius, describes the depths of their depravity and perversion:

> Tiberius, grim, paranoid, and with a taste for [depraved practices of pedophilia]; Caligula, lamenting that the Roman people did not have a single neck, so that he might cut it through; Nero, kicking his pregnant wife to death, and marrying a eunuch; and raising a pleasure palace over the fire-gutted center of Rome.[77]

---

[76] https://www.gotquestions.org/Koine-Greek.html.

[77] Quoted by William Dalrymple, "The Gangsters of Rome: The Brutal Side of the Ancient City," in "The New Statesman," November 24, 2015.

The people of Rome had descended into a mode of life as characterized by the poet Juvenal who lived in the time of the apostles. Juvenal wrote of the Romans:

The people who once upon a time bestowed military commands, high civil offices, legions, and everything else, now restrains itself, and instead, eagerly hopes for just two things: bread and circuses.[78]

Gregory S. Aldrete explains: "The 'bread' that Juvenal refers to was the free monthly grain dole that citizens of the capital city were eligible to collect, and the 'circuses' were violent public spectacles, such as gladiator games in the amphitheater and chariot races staged in the enormous racetrack called the Circus Maximus."[79]

In the Roman Colosseum, 50,000 people enjoyed seeing gladiators fight to the death in deliberately prolonged contests. They relished seeing hungry animals such as bears and tigers fight other animals like rhinos and giraffes. The beasts sometimes fought gladiators. At other times, ravenous animals were allowed to attack and eat a live human being tied to a stake. In ancient Rome, death had become a form of entertainment, live and in living color.

The good news of Christ, the apostles, and the early Christians radiated like the rays of the Hope Diamond against such a stygian background.

Born of a Woman

In a verse packed with the fundamentals of the faith such as the preexistence of the Son; with the deity of Christ ("God sent forth His Son") Paul also proclaims the humanity of Christ ("born

---

[78] Juvenal, Satires, 10:77–81.

[79] Gregory S. Aldrete, "Ancient Rome, Modern Science Fiction, and the Art of Political Distraction," Film History: An Interdisciplinary Journal, Vol. 51, Number 2, Winter 2021, 20–21.

of a woman"). Another cardinal doctrine expressed with "born of a woman" is the virgin birth of the Savior. Further packing doctrine into the sentence, Paul turns the reader's attention back to Eden when God gave the grace-filled promise of the coming of the Deliverer who would be the seed of a woman (Gen 3:15).

Under the Law

The student of the Scriptures notes that God sent His Son during the time when Israel was living in the Dispensation of the Law, an important historical notation. For example, there are those who use Luke 11:42 to put believers today under the tithe specified in the Old Testament:

> But woe to you Pharisees! For you pay tithe of mint and rue and every *kind of* garden herb, and *yet* disregard justice and the love of God; but these are the things you should have done without neglecting the others.

As they view this text, they point to Jesus' words, "These things you should have done," that is, "You should tithe."

However, this sets 2 Corinthians 9:6–7 on a collision course with the mandatory tithe of the Old Testament. Paul encourages the Corinthian believers in their giving:

> Now this *I say*, he who sows sparingly will also reap sparingly, and he who sows bountifully will also reap bountifully. Each one *must do* just as he has purposed in his heart, not grudgingly or under compulsion, for God loves a cheerful giver.

Paul's instructions to believers about grace-giving do not mesh with the Law's tithing commands. Under the Law, there was no giving as a Jew "purposed in his heart." Giving in the Grace Dispensation is not compatible with Israel's giving under the compulsion of the Law.

Tom Constable explains 2 Corinthians 9:6–7:

111

The example of the harvest suggests that the farmer has the freedom to plant as much or as little as he chooses (cf. Acts 11:29; 1 Cor 16:2). One should give generously, freely, and deliberately.

We should not give 'reluctantly' feeling that we hate to part with what we are giving. We should not give 'under compulsion,' because we feel that there is no alternative or because we think that others will look down on us if we fail to give (cf. Acts 5:1–11). We should not give impulsively or thoughtlessly either, but with inward resolve. We should give cheerfully, or hilariously, in the sense of very joyfully, but not in the sense of thoughtlessly. "Cheerful" (*hilaron*) givers always receive God's loving approval.[80]

In the Lukan text, Christ, under the Law, speaking to Jews under the Law, would, in conformity with the Law, say, "These things you should have done." Just as the system of the priesthood with the animal sacrifices under the Law, has been abolished, so has the mandatory tithing system.

Verse 5

Redemption from the Law, Adoption as Sons

"So that" (*hina*) introduces the first of two purposes for God's sending His Son. The first purpose is to "redeem" (*exagorazó*), an intensive word that packs a powerful punch, having an impact so strong that one English word does not do it justice. Thayer defines the word as

> a payment of a price to recover [someone] from the power of another, to ransom, buy off... metaphorically, of Christ

---

[80]Thomas Constable, "2 Corinthians 9:6–7," Soniclight, https://www.planobiblechapel.org/tcon/notes/html/nt/2corinthians/.2corinthians.htm.

freeing men [the Jews] from the dominion of the Mosaic law at the price of his vicarious death.[81]

Then, using the second instance of "so that," Paul uses, "we" in reference to both Jews' and gentiles' being unified in their adoption as mature sons, not immature children in the present dispensation.

Verse 6

The Spirit Crying Abba, Father

Paul lists three results of believers' maturity, the first being that they have the Holy Spirit whom God sent into the hearts of all believers. "Sent" contains the root word of "apostle," one sent forth on a mission (*exapostelló*). As a result of this mature relationship, the believer, just as the Holy Spirit, can have an intimate relationship with God the Father as evidenced by the noun, of direct address, "*Abba.*"

Unfortunately, *Abba* among many Bible teachers is trivialized to mean "Daddy" which is light years away from its meaning. Even a believer with no knowledge of the meaning of the word instinctively avoids addressing God as "Daddy." To him, it "just does not seem right," and rightly so. *Thayer's* puts it this way: "[*Abba*] is to be explained by the fact that the Chaldee, through frequent use in prayer, gradually acquired the nature of a most sacred proper name,"[82] To our English ears, "Daddy" is far below "Father" on the list of sacred titles, if it would appear at all. There is no one English word which would indicate the intimacy and reverence involved in *abba* without sounding to the English ear as sacrilegious.

---

[81] Thayer, 220.

[82] Thayer, 1.

Verse 7

No Longer a Slave, but a Son

The second result of this maturity is that the believer is no longer a slave hemmed in on every side by the Mosaic law as a Jew, nor as a pagan trapped within paganism's ceremonies and idol worship. With these results, Paul is asking the Galatians, "Why would you want to go under the immaturity of the Law system?"

If A Son, Then an Heir

The position of a slave did not include an inheritance, but a son is an heir. The inheritance of the believer is salvation. Based on these three benefits, it would be an act of stupidity to place oneself under the Mosaic law.

GALATIANS 4:8–11

*However at that time, when you did not know God, **you** were slaves to those which by nature are no gods. [9] But now that you have come to know God, or rather to be known by God, how is it that you turn back again to the weak and worthless elemental things, to which you desire to be enslaved all over again? [10] You observe **days and months and seasons and years.** [11] I fear for you, that **perhaps I have labored over you in vain**.*

Having focused on the Jews, Paul now turns the floodlights on the former plight of the gentile believers.

Verse 8

Slaves to Those that Are Not Gods

In a procession of one "you" after another (eight times in four verses), he shines a light on the-used-to-be of the Gentile believers. The basic principle of their relationship to their sixty-seven gods and goddesses is summarized by the Latin, *do ut des*, "I give that you may give." If the Romans performed their meticulous rituals, ceremonies, and sacrifices with precision, and made good on their vows, good fortune such as plentiful harvests and protection from evil spirits, from those unknown forces around them would come. Theirs was a religion of incessant awe and terror.

For ordinary Romans, religion was a part of daily life. Each home had a household shrine at which prayers and libations to the family's domestic deities were offered. Neighborhood shrines and sacred places such as springs and groves dotted the city. The Roman calendar was structured around religious observances. Women, slaves, and children all participated in a range of religious activities.[83]

Verses 9–10

Weak and Worthless Things

Paul gives the blunt and biblical viewpoint of religion in three words, the first of which is "weak" (*asthenés*). This described those who were sick, infirm, powerless or without strength. In this context, religion is powerless to result in a right standing before God. Paul continues to bluntly describe the desperate situation of the gentiles with the word, *ptóchos*, "worthless," which pictures a person "cowering, crouching down, a beggar."[84] The word for "elemental things" (*stoicheion*) is described above in verse 3.

Desire to be Enslaved Again?

Paul asks a rhetorical question to make the reader think about the disaster involved in turning to the Law. As *Thayer's Lexicon* renders this word in the Greek as "desire" *(theló)*. It speaks of a "resolve" or a "determination."

"Religion" comes from the Latin word, *religare,* "to bind." In this case, their going to the Mosaic law would bind them to the observance of *days* (the Sabbaths), *months* (the new moon festival), *seasons* (the Jewish festivals), *years*, (the Sabbatical Year), and the Year Jubilee.[85]

To be consistent, if they placed themselves under just one command of the Law for justification, they must shackle themselves with the duties of the days, months, seasons, and years

---

[83] Michael Grant, "Roman Religion," *Britannia*, June 7, 2024. https://www.britannica.com/topic/Roman-religion.

[84] Thayer, 285.

[85] Fruchtenbaum, *Faith Alone*, 39.

of the Jewish calendar. Going back to the first chapter, a person would have to be "bewitched" to do such a thing.

Verse 11

Labored Over You in Vain

Paul brings to the attention of the Galatians the fact that when he was with them, he "labored" (κεκοπίακα) over them. This word is intensive in that it signifies working to the point of fatigue, which Paul did, not for himself but for their benefit.

Having invested time and toil while in Galatia seeking to bring the Galatian believers to maturity, are they now reverting to elementary school? If so, Paul says that his exhausting work would be "in vain," that is, if they go under the Law, Paul's efforts will have been for nothing. That's how serious this issue is.

GALATIANS 4:12-16

*I beg of you, brethren, **become as I am**, for **I also have become as you are**. You have done me no wrong;* [13] *but you know that it was because of **a bodily illness** that I **preached the gospel** to you the first time;* [14] *and that which was a trial to you in my bodily condition you did not despise or loathe, but **you received me as an angel of God**, as Christ Jesus Himself.* [15] *Where then is that sense of blessing you had? For I bear you witness that, if possible, **you would have plucked out your eyes** and given them to me.* [16] *So **have I become your enemy** by telling you the truth?*

Verse 12

Thus far, Paul's argument has been professorial. Now he steps from behind his lectern for an up-close, emotional, and fatherly appeal to his children in the faith. Aristotle called this *pathos*, the stirring of the audience's emotions.

Become as I Am

Second Corinthians 3, Romans 10, and Hebrews 7, all declare that the believer is not under the Law.

Based on a later text in Galatians, some hold that the believers in Galatia had lost their salvation but this text argues to the contrary because Paul calls them "brethren." This is not the only use of "brethren;" he addresses them as his brothers in Christ eight other times, scattering the word from start to finish. Paul, being other-centered, begs his readers to enjoy what he's been enjoying since he trusted Christ: freedom!

I Also Have Become as You Are

When Paul freed himself from the Law, he became as those to whom he's writing—a gentile, no longer observing the days, months, and years of the Law. He tells them that what he has written to them is not a personal issue. He is not resentful of them or seeking revenge. Ultimately, they have grieved the Holy Spirit (Eph 4:30).

Verse 13

A Bodily Illness, Opportunity to Preach

When the Galatians first met Paul, it was evident that something was wrong with him physically; he had some kind of appearance-altering disease (*astheneia*). There has been much conjecture as to the malady. There is one definite hint found in 4:15 as to its diagnosis.

The author of the *Expositor's Greek Testament* comments:

I gather that the eyesight was imperiled by a virulent attack of ophthalmia. That disease was notoriously prevalent in the lowlands of Pamphylia through which he had been traveling, and if so contracted, would produce the symptoms described.

It incapacitated the patient for travel, produced disfigurement and offensive symptoms, but allowed free intercourse with those around him. His success in winning the hearts of those who visited him in his sick chamber suggests a chronic ailment prolonged for a considerable time, as does also the complete change in his plans.

Whatever the issue was, the attack canceled Paul's planned itinerary so that, if necessity, he had to stop and remain in Galatia. Paul's serious health issue does mesh with what the faith healers say as they poison the airwaves, their CDs, and their books with false teaching and spurious hopes as witness these quotes from a daily devotional:

God wants you well! Did you know that? He wants you healthy and strong in every single area of your life.

He wants your body to be well. He wants you free from the bondages of pain, sickness and care. Free from the worries and woes of this earthly life.

Your heavenly Father wants you well!

He needs you well. He needs you living in victory and healing so that you can teach others how to do it too. Jesus gave Himself in death so that we could be well. He was raised in life, ever making intercession for us now so that we can be well. And He wants us to be healthy and strong as a witness in these last days to a world that's filled with terror—a witness of His love, His grace and His power.[86]

Evidently, Paul had not read Ken's "Daily Devotional."

Strikingly, Paul redeemed the time of this unexpected interruption to preach the gospel from which new churches blossomed from Galatian soil.

Verse 14

You Received Me as an Angel of God

This disease produced a visual disfigurement, but the Galatians did the unusual; they did not turn away. Instead, they "received" him (*dechomai*). They did not refuse contact or friendship with him. Paul, remembering their warm welcome, says it was as if they were welcoming an angelic visitor or even the Messiah Himself, that is, with joy.

---

[86] Kenneth Copeland, "From Faith to Faith—Daily Devotional," https://www.kcm.org/read/faith-to-faith/01/27?language_content_entity=en-US.

Verse 15

You Would have Plucked out Your Eyes

Today, organ transplant from one person to another is seen as an act of superior love. That is Paul's picture of the love they had for him and how much they valued him and his ministry. When the five senses are considered—hearing, vision, touch, smell, and taste—vision is perhaps the most precious. In this analogy, Paul is saying that they considered their bond with him their most precious possession. But that was not the case now.

The loss of a friendship in the bond of Christ is a painful thing. Paul experienced such painful losses later in his ministry. (cf. 2 Tim 4:10, 16)

Verse 16

Have I become Your Enemy?

Something has put enmity between Paul and the Galatians. *Hoste,* often used as "therefore" in the Pauline corpus, introduces an affirmative conclusion. Thus, the sentence would be a statement of fact, "I am therefore become an enemy to you." This would fit with the context which indicates that there is some type of adversarial relationship between the apostle and the Galatians.

Paul attributes the deterioration of their relationship to something he said ("because I told you the truth"). Paul is not shy about using strong language in his passionate defense of the gospel.[87] He must be referring to some strong language he used during his recent visit in defending grace and denouncing the legalists, language that had been offensive to the Galatians.

---

[87] Cf. 1:6, 8–9; 3:1, 3; 5:12

GALATIANS 4:17–20

*They **eagerly** seek you, **not commendably**, but they wish to shut you out so that you will seek them. [18] But it is good always to be eagerly sought in a commendable manner, and not only when I am present with you. [19]**My children**, with whom **I am again in labor** until Christ is formed in you— [20] but I could wish to be present with you now and to **change my tone**, for I am **perplexed** about you.*

Verses 17–18

There is a principle in the book of Proverbs that the false teachers are violating. In Proverbs 16:28, Solomon writes, "A perverse man spreads strife, And a slanderer separates intimate friends."

Eagerly

The legalists are eager (*zēlousin,* "to be heated," "to boil") to draw the Galatians to their side. Paul has judged their nefarious motivation to be that driving a wedge between the Galatian believers and Paul, to "shut them out" from the apostle who won them to Christ and taught them the ways of Christ. This is a serious matter because to shut them away from Paul is to remove them from the influence of the life, teaching and writings of Paul.

Not Commendably

Eagerly seeking someone is not necessarily a bad thing; it can be commendable as in Titus 2:13–14,

Looking for the blessed hope and the appearing of the glory of our great God and Savior, Christ Jesus, who gave Himself for us to redeem us from every lawless deed, and to purify for Himself a people for His own possession, zealous for good deeds.

Paul tells them that it's always a good thing to be sought for a good cause based on a good motivation whether Paul is with them or not. But the motivation of the legalists is not good. Their motivation is selfish.

Verses 19

My Children

The verse begins with a tender tone, "my children" (*tekna*), a word denoting a little child completely and willingly dependent on another. This word is proof that he bears them no ill will as *tekna* denotes endearment. Paul's use of the word is dramatic: it's the only time in all his letters that he addresses any group or any person in such a way. His quill throbs with emotion from the start.

Paul accurately calls them his little children because he led them to Christ and then began the process of discipleship, child-training in the faith. This implies that the legalists who are leading them astray are not their spiritual fathers; they had nothing to do with their being born again. They are interlopers who have kidnapped the Galatians from their parent.

Am I Again in Labor

All the progress Paul had made in the discipleship process has now ceased. It's impossible for the Mosaic law to bring the child to maturity. His next statement is the plaintive, "Do I have to start the discipleship process all over again to enable you to see that faith alone is all that is necessary for mature Christian living?"

123

Verse 20

Change My Tone

Paul desires to be with them so he can change his tone and speak to them up close and personal. In this way, they can sense the nuances of his argument and his tone of voice. His desire is not the wish of a pedantic to gather data for an article in a scholarly journal; it's that of a shepherd whose heart beats for his flock.

Perplexed

Paul is so frustrated with the Galatians that he says, "I am perplexed with you." By this, the apostle is showing his frustration with the Galatians to the point that, "I do not know how to deal with you (*aporoumai*)! He places the "perplexed" in the middle voice which is used to describe actions that the subject performs on itself or is affected by in a reflexive or reciprocal sense. The middle voice is often used to convey a sense of involvement or interest on the part of the subject in the action.

The apostle is perplexed because he's dealing with irrationality on steroids—what freed slaves would willingly go back to slavery? Who would go back to what Paul called, "a ministry of death"?

The importance of discipleship training in grace for the new believer is clear in Paul's anguish over the young believers in Galatia. Often, evangelistic efforts simply lead someone to Christ, include him in a monthly report of the number of converts, then abandon the spiritual baby to be tossed to and fro by every wind of doctrine for the rest of his life and thereby becoming fodder for cults.

AN ILLUSTRATION: BOND & FREE

GALATIANS 4:21–31

GALATIANS 4:21–23

Tell me, you who want to be under law, do you not listen to the law? [22] *For it is written that Abraham had two sons, one by the bondwoman and one by the free woman.* [23] *But the son by the bondwoman was born according to the flesh, and the son by the free woman through the promise.*

Verse 21

Tell Me

A present imperative begins this section: "Tell me." The word is cast in the present tense which indicates the starting and continuance of an action. Paul is beginning a long-distance discussion with them by asking for their response to a perceptive question: "Do you not comprehend (*akouete*) the Law?"

Listen

His question takes the modern reader back to examinations in his formative school days during which he would be tested, not only on his ability to read the words of a text but also his ability to understand what he's reading.

For the Galatians, it's time to go back to the Bible and comprehend the saga of Abraham, Sarah, Hagar, Ishmael, and Isaac that begins in Genesis 16.

The Galatians must realize what going back into bondage means. In a sense, Pastor Paul is saying, "Let's think this through." He begins by submitting for their consideration an allegory based on an event famous in Jewish history.

Verses 22–23

It is Written

The tense of "It is written" is an important tense in bibliology because it's in the perfect tense which carries two ideas: (1) completed action and (2) the continuing results of that action. The action of the writing of Genesis 16 was completed at some time in the past, and the results of that writing continue up to the present. Therefore, what Paul is saying is, "It stands written!"

Paul writes in 2 Timothy 1:12, "…for I know whom I have believed." He puts "believed" in the perfect tense to signify he believed in the past (AD 34) with the results of that belief continuing up to the moment of his writing that sentence in the fall of AD 67[88]

The Bondwoman and the Free Woman

The argument proceeds by the masterful contrasting of slavery as opposed to liberty. Paul does so by citing the history of Abraham and comparing him to the individual believer. God had made a seemingly impossible promise to the patriarch: "I will give you a son." This promise brought up a question: How?

The question was, "By the flesh or by faith?" The answer of Abraham was, "By flesh," i.e., works. This is where Hagar enters the historical record. Abraham and Hagar, the bondswoman, would produce the promised heir.

The result was Ishmael. Abraham had chosen wrongly as opposed to waiting in faith on God to fulfill His promise. As Paul proceeds, Abraham's plan (suggested by Sarah) to use the bondwoman availed nothing.

---

[88] Donald A. Carson and Douglas J. Moo, *An Introduction to the New Testament*, 2nd ed. (Grand Rapids: Zondervan, 2005), 578.

In the analogy, a person has the promise of eternal life. The question is the same as Abraham's: "How?" A person has the same two options as Abraham: by works (in the Galatian context, this would be keeping the Law) with the result of death, or the by-faith option which would produce a right standing before God and, therefore, eternal life.

GALATIANS 4:24–27

*This is **allegorically speaking**, for these women are two covenants: one proceeding from Mount Sinai bearing children who are to be slaves; she is Hagar. ²⁵ Now this **Hagar is Mount Sinai in Arabia** and corresponds to the present Jerusalem, for she is in slavery with her children. ²⁶ **But the Jerusalem above is free; she is our mother.** ²⁷ For it is written, "Rejoice, barren woman who does not bear; Break forth and shout, you who are not in labor; For more numerous are the children of the desolate Than of the one who has a husband."*

Verse 24

Allegorically Speaking

An allegory "consists of extended metaphors or figures that represent or symbolize certain truths or concepts. An allegory, to summarize, describes a larger narrative episode that has features laden with symbolic function."[89]

The reader of this extended text must not think that Paul is using the allegorical method of interpretation which would declare that Abraham, Sarah, Hagar, Ismael, and Isaac were not literal, historical people. He is taking a historical account and drawing spiritual applications from it to teach truth. "This was a Jewish way of quoting the Old Testament in that period."[90]

---

[89] Brent E. Parker, "Typology And Allegory: Is There A Distinction? A Brief Examination Of Figural Reading," *Southern Baptist Journal of Theology* 21:1 (Spring 17), 57.

[90] Fruchtenbaum, Israelology: The Missing Link in Systematic Theology, 843.

The most famous book in English literature, the classic, *Pilgrim's Progress,* is the second most-read book in the English language after the Bible. It is an allegory from beginning to end. Spurgeon claimed to have read it at least one hundred times!

The protagonist is Pilgrim but he's not a literal person. In the story, Pilgrim meets Mr. Great-heart, Pliable, Obstinate, and Worldly Wiseman, none of whom existed in space and time.

The allegorical method of interpretation, when applied to biblical accounts, deliteralizes the history of the narrative to the point where it is not taken as actual events. A case in point would be the account of Jonah in the stomach of the great fish. According to liberal critics, the prophet's being in the fish is deliteralized to become Jonah's being in the darkness of depression.

Or other critics say that Jonah is Israel, the large fish is the Babylonian world power that swallowed up Israel. It is easily seen that the Bible becomes elastic and can be made to mean what each interpreter says it means. The results are a train wreck with ten different interpreters giving ten different meanings to any given text. The man in the pew leaves the auditorium bewildered.

Origen (ca. AD 185—ca. AD 253), a church father who will live in infamy, infected the church with the allegorical method of interpretation. The Reformers fought against this hermeneutic to bring the church back to the literal, historical, and grammatical hermeneutic of Christ and the apostles, but they did not employ the literal method in reference to prophecy.

Origen was not the only church father who infected the church. Augustine (AD 354–430) used the allegorical method to "enhance our understanding" of the parable of The Good Samaritan in Luke 10:25–37.

A certain man went down from Jerusalem to Jericho; Adam himself is meant; Jerusalem is the heavenly city of peace, from whose blessedness Adam fell; Jericho means the moon, and signifies our mortality, because it is born, waxes, wanes, and dies. Thieves are the devil and his angels. Who stripped him, namely, of his immortality; and beat him, by persuading

130

him to sin; and left him half-dead, because in so far as man can understand and know God, he lives, but in so far as he is wasted and oppressed by sin, he is dead; he is therefore called half-dead.

The priest and the Levite who saw him and passed by, signify the priesthood and ministry of the Old Testament which could profit nothing for salvation. Samaritan means Guardian, and therefore the Lord Himself is signified by this name.

The binding of the wounds is the restraint of sin. Oil is the comfort of good hope; wine the exhortation to work with fervent spirit. The beast is the flesh in which He deigned to come to us. The being set upon the beast is belief in the incarnation of Christ. The inn is the Church, where travelers returning to their heavenly country are refreshed after pilgrimage. The morrow is after the resurrection of the Lord.

The two pence are either the two precepts of love, or the promise of this life and of that which is to come. The innkeeper is the Apostle. The supererogatory payment is either his counsel of celibacy, or the fact that he worked with his own hands lest he should be a burden to any of the weaker brethren when the Gospel was new, though it was lawful for him "to live by the gospel.

Modern examples of allegorizing abound in pulpits today: the David and Goliath conflict becomes ways to confront one's giant problems. (No. This was David's first step toward the throne.) A blasphemous example of allegorizing was an Easter sermon on the resurrection allegorized into, "Jesus had a comeback, and you can have a comeback from your problems today."

Thus, Paul's use of allegory is to remind his Jewish readers of an important event in their history regarding Abraham, Sarah, Hagar, and Ishmael from which he will make a spiritual application.

131

Verse 25

Hagar is Mount Sinai

In Paul's comparison, Hagar is the Mosaic law, Ishmael is legalism, Mt. Sinai is the place where the Israelites agreed to their bondage, The Old Jerusalem is the Jerusalem, the one in Paul's day. That Jerusalem is now in slavery is now in double slavery: to Rome and to the Law.

Verse 26

Jerusalem Above is Free, Our Mother

Sarah is the Abrahamic covenant; Isaac is justification through the promise. The New Jerusalem is free. Her destiny is to appear with the Son. There are two sonships: the slavery of the Law refers to the children of Hagar in bondage; those who exercise faith are the sons of Abraham. The Jerusalem above is the home of all believers. The problem with the Galatians is that they're following the wrong son of Abraham, Ishmael, who has led them into slavery! Any pastor who is encouraging his flock into a works system for justification is an Ishmael.

Verse 27

Isaiah 54 Quotation

Paul brings to the reader's attention Isaiah 54, a prophecy that he applies to Sarah. She will have, not only a son, but also "numerous children," that is, all true believers, including Christians.

GALATIANS 4:28–31

And you brethren, **like Isaac, are children of promise.**
[29] *But as at that time* he who was born according to the flesh persecuted him who was born according to the Spirit, so it is now also. *[30] But what does the Scripture say?* **"Cast out the bondwoman and her son, For the son of the bondwoman shall not be an heir with the son of the free woman."** *[31] So then, brethren, we are not children of a bondwoman, but* **of the free woman.**

Verse 28

Like Isaac, Children of Promise

The Holy Spirit carries Paul along to his conclusion of this section in verses 28–31.

All believers follow in the line of the miraculously fulfilled promise of God in the person of Isaac, born according to the covenant God made to Abraham, a husband well beyond his child-bearing years. His baby was born free; he was not a slave. At the time of faith alone, the believer is born again, according to the promise of God; he is free from the Law.

Verse 29

The Flesh-Born Persecuted the Spirit-Born

Paul unrolls his mental scroll to Genesis 21 to behavior unacceptable in any family: a child "harassing" (*ediōken*, imperfect tense, repeated action) his stepbrother. In the Hebrew account, the word *tsachaq* means "to laugh at," "to make sport of," thus, "to mock."

133

What makes this bullying doubly intolerable is that Ishmael was fourteen years older than Isaac. Abraham's lack of faith wreaked havoc within the family and it was Sarah who realized what was happening, not Abraham. Mothers seem to have more insight into family relationships.

So It Is Now Also

It is self-evident that legalism persecutes and mocks grace. Those who insist that works are necessary for earning a right standing before God often become infuriated when a believer declares with Isaiah that legalism is as filthy rags. The legalist becomes upset when hearing that there is only one way to God, the by-faith way, and that all religions with their prescribed works are not the way to God.

Verse 30

Genesis 21 Quotation

Paul draws from Genesis 21 and God's approval of Sarah's telling her husband that Hagar and Ishmael must go for the safety of the family.

Paul directs the Galatians to take the same action God directed Abraham to do: to expel the false teachers.

Paul gives additional guidance in Titus 1:10–11 concerning those of the circumcision: "For there are many rebellious men, empty talkers and deceivers, especially those of the circumcision, who must be silenced because they are upsetting whole families, teaching things they should not *teach* for the sake of sordid gain."

Bradley Maston rightly comments about the silencing of "those of the circumcision:"

The original text is a command—an imperative. It is something that absolutely must be done for the local church to magnify Christ on this earth. This is like a teacher in a classroom, or a judge in a court of law, commanding someone to be silent at once! The Greek word here is *epistomizo…* literally, it would read, "Cover their mouths." or 'Shove something into their mouths.' The picture of shoving a piece of cloth in a person's mouth, the putting duct-tape over it is not too extreme a picture of this concept.[91]

Verse 31

Children of the Free Woman

Paul concludes the strongest defense of salvation by faith alone (chapters 3–4) in all inspired literature. In word pictures, in biblical quotations, and in historical events he has woven a masterpiece demonstrating the incompatibility of faith and works as methods of obtaining justification.

The false apostles were trying to get the Galatians to submit to the Mosaic pattern to earn eternal life from God. This approach is not grace, which declares that people cannot earn God's favor but must rely on God to deliver what He has promised, eternal life through faith alone in Christ alone!

---

[91] Bradley W. Maston, *Titus: Life in the Church* (Tacoma, WA: True Grace Books, 2024), 29.

PRACTICAL MATTERS

GALATIANS 5:1–6:10

GALATIANS 5:1–6

*It was for freedom that **Christ set us free**; therefore **keep standing firm** and **do not be subject again to a yoke of slavery**. [2] **Behold I, Paul**, say to you that if **you receive circumcision**, Christ will be of **no benefit to you**. [3] And **I testify again** to every man who receives circumcision, that he is under **obligation to keep the whole Law**. [4] You have been **severed from Christ**, you who are seeking to be justified by law; you have fallen from grace. [5] For **we through the Spirit**, by faith, are waiting for the hope of righteousness. [6] For **in Christ Jesus neither circumcision nor uncircumcision** means anything, but **faith working through love**.*

Verse 1

Christ Set Us Free

This may be said to be the keystone verse of the book as it's what holds the great truths of the epistle together. It is a summary statement that looks back to the previous four chapters and looks forward to the next two.

Christ's death set us free (*ēleutherōsen*, aorist tense, at a point in time) from the Law. His death did not set free from a few commands of the Law; He did not only set us free from a section of the Law such as the so-called "ceremonial parts in the Law," but He set the believer free from the entire Law.

Romans 10:4 declares that Christ is the end of the Law, all its 613 commands. This includes the Ten Commandments to which Paul refers as the written-on-stone part of the Law.

It was a sad day in church history when Calvin and many of the Reformers, believing that the ceremonial laws (e.g., animal sacrifices, dietary restrictions, feast days, etc.) were no longer binding on Christians because of the death of Christ, said that the moral laws (the Ten Commandments) are still binding. They said that God has done away with the moral laws only in the sense that they no longer condemn.

But in that declaration, Calvin had a problem: if the Ten Commandments are all still binding on believers, why have Christians throughout history met to worship on Sunday rather than on Saturday?

Another seemingly insurmountable problem has to do with consistency in reference to binding the church under the yoke of the Law. That is, most of the Ten Commandments carried the death penalty for the violator, yet that ultimate penalty has not been carried over into the church age by those who would make the Ten Commandments binding today. A law without a penalty is no law at all.

And what about the Law that required two eyewitnesses to a murder before the imposition of capital punishment? This eliminates the prosecution's presenting circumstantial evidence and DNA. The Mosaic law, in its entirety, was for Israel and Israel alone for that one specific period in history that ended at the cross.

Keep Standing Firm

"Standing firm" (*stēkete*) is one of the defenses against legalism. Paul casts the word as a present imperative, i.e., "start standing firm and continue to do so!" The Galatian believers were to maintain their allegiance to freedom.

Not Subject Again to A Yoke of Slavery

To become subject (*enechesthe*, "entangled," or "ensnared") is to be held captive by the Law.

Paul will later hear Peter use the figure of a yoke to describe the Mosaic law at the Jerusalem Council recorded in Acts 15. This is a negative word picture of bearing a heavy burden, and a yoke was also a means of controlling an animal. Just so, the Law controlled the diet, the clothing, the sanitation, the offerings (tithing), even home-building (Deut 22:8), and the agricultural practices of the Jews.

The legalists were putting a heavy yoke on the believers. Think of the yoke works for salvation is: the yoke of "am I doing enough?" The yoke of "am I doing it long enough?" The yoke of "is what I'm doing good enough?" No wonder Paul and Peter chose that word because it presents a graphic word picture of the burdensome entanglement the Law carries with it.

Verse 2

Behold I, Paul

Paul begins with a lively command, *idou,* "Look!" "See!" He is saying, "Listen to what I'm going to say!" He's stressing his authority as an apostle on a mission from and for Christ, "I, Paul."

If You Receive Circumcision

The Greek language had a precise way of saying things. Paul provides an example of this in his use of the word *if.* He structures the sentence using a third-class condition which denotes, "Maybe you will or maybe you will not receive circumcision." There were those who had not joined the legalists. He's using the rite of circumcision to stand for the Mosaic law. There were some who were considering being enslaved. They have yet to make this momentous decision, so Paul appeals to them to listen carefully to him.

No Benefit to You

They have been justified by faith but if they put themselves under the Law, they will be bereft of the ministry of the Holy Spirit because His indwelling was not provided by trying to keep the Law.

The very act of circumcision means that they've come to believe that their salvation depends on faith plus works and that their sanctification depends on their putting on the yoke of works.

If they hoist the yoke around their necks, they certainly will not lose their salvation, but they will lose their joy in the enabling power of the Holy Spirit; the burden of the yoke will grieve and quench His vital ministry (Eph 4:30; 1 Thess 5:19).

To grieve the Holy Spirit is to bring pain or sorrow to Him, words that show the third Person of the Trinity is a *he*, not an *it*. The believer can grieve the Holy Spirit by committing any of the sins in the context, by unwholesome words instead of speech that build up and encourage. Grieving and quenching the Spirit are used synonymously.

To enter the entanglement of the Law would be a tacit denial of faith alone for salvation and sanctification. It is no wonder that Paul began the sentence with, "Look!"

Verse 3

I Testify Again

Marturomai ("I testify") signifies that a solemn declaration is coming. As the observant reader knows, this is not the first time that Paul speaks bluntly about the result of being circumcised.

Obligation to Keep the Whole Law

The command to be circumcised comes, like the Greeks bearing gifts, but as a husbandman carrying a yoke.

In Vergil's *Aeneid,* the Greeks deceived the Trojans by leaving behind the Trojan Horse they had built, containing some of their soldiers, unknown to the Trojans. One of the Trojans, upon seeing the surmised "gift," said, "I fear the Greeks, even bearing gifts." The Trojans looked upon it as a gift and took it inside their walls. When the night came, the Greek soldiers came out of the horse, opened the gates of Troy, and let their army in.

The command to be circumcised will be accompanied by 612 other burdens. The rite of circumcision, as an act of law-keeping for justification, places the Jew under an obligation regarding the other 612 commands, and Paul describes that obligation as "bound to some duty" (*opheilétes*).[92]

To choose to keep only one law for a right standing before God binds a person to all the others. In any system of the law of the land, a citizen cannot decide which laws he will keep and which he will break. "The law" is singular but there is a multiplicity of laws wrapped up in "the law." That "multicity" means "the whole Law" (cf. Rom 7:2, 6).

The believer is free from being obligated to keep the Mosaic law, in part or in whole. Once justified by faith alone, the obligation to keep the Law is wiped off the books.

Verse 4

This text has scared many believers out of their security and thereby, their assurance of salvation. Carolyn Moore, using the illustration of a child holding his parent's hand as they negotiate traffic, writes about the Wesleyan view salvation:

> God gives it, but we have to accept it. By the same token, God walks us through the journey of salvation, inviting us to work it out daily with fear and trembling, but at every point on the way we must make the choice to keep our hand in His.
>
> ...So what about that 'blessed assurance' we always sing about? Is it so blessed after all? Is there really any assurance? Absolutely! ...Assurance is the promise that with your submission and surrender, God will get you safely through

---

[92] Thayer, 469.

the traffic to the other side. Our decision to simply rest our hand in His—to submit to His will. That is all that's required, and that is only a struggle if we choose it to be." [93]

Moore's definition of blessed assurance is not blessed because it floats on a vast sea of subjectivity with three questions: the quality of the submission, the duration of the submission, and the extent of the submission (all His will, or part of His will, for how long?).

Such "assurance," based on the strength of holding on, would mean a life lived in perpetual fear whenever those questions surface. Each question would be like trying to hold three beach balls simultaneously under water—they would always be breaking for the surface.

Severed From Christ

Paul points out the serious situation of those who have gone back under the Law: by the severing, they "have rendered Christ inactive, inoperative" (*katērgēthēte*). This is a statement of relationship, not the issue of salvation. To go back to the Law for justification or sanctification would render their relationship to Christ inoperative/inactive.

By not having an active and growing relationship with Christ, they have "fallen from grace." To choose the Law method of salvation automatically means that they have "fallen from grace, they are now operating in the realm of Law."

If they had lost their salvation Paul would have never called them "brothers" nor would he have written, "Because you are sons, God has sent forth the Spirit of His Son into our hearts,

---

[93] Carolyn Moore, "What Wesleyans Believe About Once Saved Always Saved," May 22, 2018, https://artofholiness.com/what-wesleyans-believe-about-once-saved-always-saved/. (Emphasis added.)

crying, 'Abba! Father!'" in Galatians 4:6. It is significant that four times after 5:4, he still refers to them as his "brothers."

There is irony in the verse; what the legalists are saying is that "To be connected and in union with Christ, you must submit to circumcision, that is, the Mosaic law," whereas Paul is saying, "No, that's what will separate you from a growing relationship with Christ."

Looking at grace and law as two spheres is helpful. To fall from grace is to leave the realm of grace for the realm of law/works. In the sphere of the Law, the *modus vivendi* is to trust works and not rely on the Holy Spirit to live the *ethos* of the Christian life.

A person cannot have one foot in Law and the other foot in grace; the two realms are antithetical and cannot be straddled. This is the problem with the papal decree that pronounced faith plus works as necessary for salvation. Roman Catholicism has one foot in law, the other in grace. The council of Trent puts forth this straddling:

> The formula for justification that Trent avows is: faith plus works begins a process that leads to justification. The Council [of Trent] clearly repudiated the concept of faith alone. It states in its Sixth Session, Chapter XVI on the fruits of justification....to those who work well unto the end and trust in God, eternal life is to be offered, both as a grace mercifully promised to the sons of God through Christ Jesus, and as a reward promised by God himself, to be faithfully given to their good works and merits.[94]

Law, "work well," and grace, "trust in God," are both present in this decree. Roman Catholics and Protestants both straddle this issue, answer the question, "Is heaven a free gift or do you have to earn it?" Too many will respond, "It's a free gift but you have

---

[94] "The Sixteenth Century Debates on Justification," https://covenantofgracechurch.org/the-sixteenth-century-debates-on-justification/.

to earn it." Such an answer is devoid of logic. It will take a lot of wood to build a bridge between their ignorance and the truth.

Verse 5

Through the Spirit

This verse begins with an explanatory *gar* ("for") immediately following verse 4. Lest the reader think that the Galatians have lost their salvation, the Holy Spirit carries Paul along to choose "we," a choice showing that both he and they, as believers, are united in faith. Paul wants them to understand something: God has already delivered on His promise of positional righteousness credited to the believer through the Holy Spirit by faith, not by the Law.

Therefore, all that God has promised the believer will, by faith, also be, by faith, be fulfilled. One of those promises yet to be fulfilled is glorification. Another of those promises is sanctification, growth by the Holy Spirit in one's ability to walk righteously according to that righteousness which already belongs to every believer legally in Christ. The believer grows in grace through dependence on the finished work of Christ, and that growth is achieved apart from the Law.

Verse 6

In Christ Jesus

Paul refers to an important doctrine in New Testament theology, that of positional truth. Through faith alone in Christ, the believer enjoys a new position, that of being forever "in Christ." The perfect righteousness of Christ is credited to his account, not experientially but by virtue of his new position (2 Cor 5:17).

Neither Circumcision Nor Uncircumcision

The rite of circumcision, so crucial for salvation according to the false teachers, in reality "has no force or strength" (*ischuó*). In fact, whether a person submits to the rite or not, means nothing; both are impotent salvifically.

Faith Working Through Love

In 1 Corinthians 15:3, Paul did not write, "For I delivered to you as of first importance what I also received, the rite of circumcision and the Mosaic law." But that's what the legalists were making of first importance. Paul said that the gospel was of first importance, namely, "that Christ died for our sins according to the Scriptures and that He was buried, and that He was raised on the third day according to the Scriptures" (1 Cor 15:3–4). Legalism takes the spotlight off Christ's person and work and shines it on some type of human effort.

What does have strength and power is faith in the substitutionary atonement of Christ. Paul was not ashamed of its power (Rom 1:16).

GALATIANS 5:7–12

*You were **running well**; who **hindered you from obeying the truth**? ⁸ **This persuasion** did not come from Him who calls you. ⁹ **A little leaven** leavens the whole lump of dough. ¹⁰ **I have confidence in you** in the Lord that you will adopt no other view; but **the one who is disturbing you will bear his judgment**, whoever he is. ¹¹ But I, brethren, **if I still preach circumcision**, why am I still persecuted? Then **the stumbling block of the cross** has been abolished. ¹² I wish that those who are troubling you would even mutilate themselves.*

Verse 7

Running Well

Paul shows his knowledge of athletics when he commends the Galatians for their previous growth, picturing them as athletes exerting themselves and striving hard (*etrechete*) toward the goal.

Hindered You from Obeying the Truth

The athletic analogy continues as Paul pictures the false teachers as impeding a runner's path by cutting off his way (*enekopsen*). In the ancient world, to compete in the games, an athlete had to be a citizen which would illustrate the Galatians as citizens of the New Jerusalem, that is, saved and secure.

Therefore, Paul is not telling the reader how to become a Christian; he is comparing the life of the believer (the citizen) to the athlete. The legalists have come into the lane of the Galatian athletes and knocked them into the infield, thereby cutting them off from spiritual development.

Verse 8

This Persuasion

God is not responsible for the conviction (*peismonē*) to which they have come. The doctrines of justification and sanctification by the Law have not come from God. God did not foreordain them nor foreordain their believing them. This false doctrine is under the rubric of 1 Timothy 4:1: "But the Spirit explicitly says that in later times some will fall away from the faith, paying attention to deceitful spirits and doctrines of demons."

Verse 9

A Little Leaven

This well-known proverb encourages the readers to think about the serious consequences for the Galatian churches. Leaven is a small portion of fermented dough which is put into a fresh lump of dough, then it spreads to the whole. The question is, to what or whom is Paul referring? Is he talking about a small number of false teachers or is he referring to a little bad doctrine?

Leaven in Scripture is always symbolic of evil (including its usage in Matt 13:33). Since God used Paul to write an entire epistle combating legalism, it's not "a little bad doctrine." Rather, Paul is referring to the fact that "very few of these Judaizing intruders are sufficient to corrupt the whole church."[95]

---

[95] *Vincent's Word Studies*, https://biblehub.com/commentaries/galatians/5–9.htm

Verse 10

I have Confidence in You

Paul begins with the emphatic, "I have confidence in you" (*ego pepoitha*). Paul firmly believes that when they finish the letter, and when they reflect on his argument, they will come to the correct conclusion and agree with him. He has shown them logically, scripturally, and biblically, there is no other alternative.

Judgment of the One Disturbing You

This fits with the leaven's being symbolic of the evil teachers ruining the churches because Paul singles them out with a dire warning. There is a heavier judgment on those who teach false doctrine: "Let not many of you become teachers, my brethren, knowing that as such we will incur a stricter judgment" (Jas 3:1).

In too many instances, churches are so in need of Sunday school teachers that they hand a neophyte believer the lessons to be taught and send him into a room of middle schoolers. On the other side of the coin, after a long meeting of trying to get someone to volunteer to teach a Sunday school class, finally a weary member volunteers, saying, "I'll do it if no one else will." To recognize a false teacher, even a few of them (one is too many) is to begin the process of ruining the church.

Verse 11

If I Still Preach Circumcision

Reading an epistle is like listening to one side of a telephone conversation with only an inkling what the other side is saying. Hearing Paul's side of the conversation, one can gather that those opposing his ministry have brought before the Galatians an accusation: that he preaches circumcision to the Jews but not to the gentiles.

Paul did request that Timothy undergo the surgery, but the reason was not for salvation but for a fruitful ministry. Timothy's mother was a Jew, his father was a gentile. To gain a hearing from the Jews, the surgery was necessary. This is called "crossing cultural lines."

In September 1855, after Hudson Taylor had served as a missionary in China for only eighteen months, he made a decision that was very radical for that era. Rather than living in a missionary compound in Shanghai and wearing European clothing, he decided to live right among the Chinese and to adopt their native dress and other amoral aspects of indigenous culture. He desired to do this in order to lessen cultural barriers to the dissemination of the Christian Gospel and to show his high regard for the native culture of those he was trying to reach.

He hired a barber to shave his head. A single shock of hair on the back of his head was preserved to be grown into a queue."[96]

This might be called "The haircut that changed China".

This accusation against Paul seems to be an example of throwing mud on the wall and seeing what sticks. Anyone could show the fallacy of it as Paul does: "If *I* am preaching circumcision, why am I being persecuted?"[97] However, this charge demonstrates just how far fallen man will go in persecuting grace, that is, into irrationality.

---

[96] Christie, Vance, "Crossing Cultural Lines to Promote the Gospel, https://vancechristie.com/2018/03/22/crossing-cultural-lines-promote-gospel-hudson-taylor/

[97] Emphasis added to reflect the Greek text.

The Stumbling Block of the Cross

The root word for "stumbling block" means "the movable stick or trigger of a trap, a trap-stick" (*skandalon*). The offense of the cross was a stumbling block to the Jews because it was offensive to them that Paul was declaring that the cross had abolished the Law. If Paul preached circumcision, that would have removed the stumbling block.

Verse 12

This verse is an example of sanctified sarcasm. Other examples of sarcasm are in 1 Kings 18:27, Isaiah 44:15–17, and 1 Corinthians 4:8–10. Paul's use of sarcasm in this verse is of the earth, earthy. In referring to the false teachers' obsession with circumcision, he says that his desire is that they not be content with that surgery, but go on to perform a complete amputation (*apokopsontai*). The Galatian readers would sense that Paul's blood is boiling (cf. Prov 8:13; Psa 97:10; Amos 5:15).

There is a proper anger as seen in Mark 3:5: "After looking around at them *with anger*, grieved at their hardness of heart, He [Jesus] said to the man, 'Stretch out your hand.' And he stretched it out, and his hand was restored."[98]

Mark is the only author who, as Peter remembers the emotion of Christ, explicitly states that Jesus was angry (*orge*, an abiding, settled habit of mind). This type of anger is proper because it is righteous indignation in the presence of unrepentant evil, described as, "hardness (*porosei*) of heart" (cf. Eph 4:26).

---

[98] Emphasis added.

GALATIANS 5:13–18

*For you were **called to freedom, brethren; only do not turn your freedom into an opportunity for the flesh**, but through love serve one another. [14] For the whole Law is fulfilled in one word, in the statement, "You shall **love your neighbor as yourself**. But if you **bite and devour one another**, take care that you are not consumed by one another." [16] **But I say, walk by the Spirit**, and you will not carry out **the desire of the flesh**. [17] **For the flesh sets its desire against the Spirit, and the Spirit against the flesh**; for these are in opposition to one another, so that you may not do the **things that you please**. [18] But If You are Led by the Spirit, You are Not Under the Law.*

Verse 13

Called to Freedom

Continuing in this section of charges that the false teachers have aimed at Paul to discredit his teaching, Paul answers a question that people have not stopped asking for over 2,000 years: "If I am saved by grace through faith, if nothing I do can cause me to lose my salvation, does that not mean that I can do anything I want?" This "gotcha" question is usually phrased around one's being given "a license to sin."

The Bible gives a terse and complete answer to this: "Absolutely not!" Romans 6:1–2 makes this clear: "What shall we say then? Are we to continue in sin so that grace may increase? May it never be! How shall we who died to sin still live in it?" "May it never be!" (*me genoito*) is an idiomatic expression meaning, "Far from it!" This "far from it" is two Greek words Paul uses to express his indignation. There are no Christians carrying the mythical license to sin. No matter what the Galatians have done, they have not lost their salvation as indicated by "brethren."

For his fellow believers, Paul defines "freedom." It is not a freedom to satisfy the desires of the still-present-with-us sin-nature (cf. 1 John 1:8). On the contrary, the biblical definition of the freedom the believer enjoys is, in context, the privilege and opportunity to love and serve one's fellow believers. This freedom to love and to serve is a long way from perverting its use for a license to indulge the selfish whims, desires, and sins of the flesh.

Verse 14

You Shall Love Your Neighbor as Yourself

Paul quotes the Mosaic law to summarize. On a personal level, if a person loves his neighbor as himself, he has fulfilled this command. The problem is, the command does not come with the love necessary to fulfill the command which is repeated in the New Testament though modified to a higher standard: "A new commandment I give to you, that you love one another, even as I have loved you, that you also love one another. By this all men will know that you are My disciples, if you have love for one another" (John 13:34–35). The Law commands the "do this" but not the ability to "do this."

The ability comes to the believer by faith through the empowerment the Holy Spirit gives to fulfill the command. Loving their fellow believers is what the Galatians are to be doing. But by putting themselves back under the Law, fulfilling the principle of the command is impossible. There is no Department of Enablement in the realm of the Law.

Verse 15

Bite and Devour One Another

Paul brings the Galatians face to face with the possibility of their committing ecclesiastical suicide. Apparently, the body of Christ, the church, had divided into two factions in the Galatian churches: the believers who advocated grace and the believers

153

who advocated law bitterly opposing one another. Paul uses "bite" (*daknó*) in the metaphorical sense, meaning, "to wound the soul with reproaches."[99] Such verbs as "bite" and "devour" describe what wild animals do to each other with the result of self-destruction as demonstrated by "devour," an intensive word, meaning, "to eat up" (*katesthiete*).

Sadly, church business meetings can erupt into believers biting and devouring one another with name-calling, angry words, and accusations, which produce scarred souls with wounds that may never heal. New members are shocked by such meetings and vow to never return to watch the wild animals at work. The world shakes its collective head.

Paul will now develop the practice of their freedom under grace on the individual level. These verses make up a course in "Living Without the Law 101."

Verse 16

But I Say

Using a conjunction of contrast, "But" (*de*), the Galatians who have been listening to the howling of the wolves are told to listen to what Paul says about this new freedom in grace.

Walk by the Spirit

A word picture is presented here for what it is like to live without the Law: walking by the Spirit. This is a picture of a believer's everyday life and the tasks therein. "Walk" is a present tense imperative (*peripateite*) which indicates, "start walking by the Holy Spirit and do so consistently."

Free from the control of the yoke of the Law, the believer is not lawless but is to be controlled by the indwelling Holy Spirit.

---

[99] Thayer, 124.

This freedom is not license but the liberty to be controlled by the Holy Spirit to love others. The license to sin argument collapses in view of the command to walk by the Spirit.

The imperative, "walk by the Spirit" is, all too often, left, like "grace," undefined, therefore vague. Socrates claimed that until you know what a thing is, you cannot answer any other questions about it. Walking by means of the Spirit needs defining.

Walking by means of the Spirit happens when the soul of the believer is Scripture-soaked. When the believer fills his soul with the word of God, the Holy Spirit can reveal to the believer's mind the previously stored Scripture as well as its application. Then, when the believer applies the Scripture, he is walking by means of the Holy Spirit. The Spirit then produces the fruit: the character of Christ. Amazing!

The imperative "walk" shows that spiritual growth is not passive; the believer is not to sit back and wait for a spiritual zapping; such growth is not automatic. This puts to rest the tired platitude, "Let go and let God."

The Desire of the Flesh

In sentence after sentence, Paul continues to say that living without the Law is not granting a sin permit. The flesh has its desire (*epithumia*, "passionate longing for what is forbidden"), but walking by the Spirit will not fulfill that desire. Paul waxes emphatic in saying, "not," as he uses the double negative *ou me* to double down on the impact. The desire of the sin nature is strong as Paul writes that its passionate longing is to see that its desire is accomplished.

The strength of the passionate longing of the flesh in the heroin addict who will rob, lie, steal, and even kill to get one more fix or the gambling addict who will urinate in the chair so as not to leave the slot machine, as one did.

Verse 17

War Between the Flesh and the Spirit

What Paul describes is a conflict in which there is no neutrality. The believer is either following his sin nature or he is following the Holy Spirit.

Barnes Notes on the Bible includes this comment on that subject:

> The inclinations and desires of the flesh are contrary to those of the Spirit. They draw us away in an opposite direction, and while the Spirit of God would lead us one way, our carnal nature would lead us another, and thus produce the painful controversy which exists in our minds. The word "Spirit" here refers to the Spirit of God, and to his influences on the heart. And these are contrary.... They are opposite in their nature. They never can harmonize...[100]

Things That You Please

The thrust of Paul's argument at this point in "Living Without the Law" is that, because of this conflict, the believer will act either by the Holy Spirit or by his carnal nature; one or the other. The upshot of this conflict is that the believer will never achieve perfection.

Verse 18

The "if" in this statement is a first-class condition in the Greek text, that is, Paul is assuming the statement is true for the sake of argument. It is true that the believer, led by the Spirit, is not under the Law. Paul is saying that the Holy Spirit leads every believer. But there's a problem: The nature of His leadership is

---

[100] https://biblehub.com/commentaries/galatians/5–17.htm

not by force. The believer may choose to be led by the Holy Spirit or to be led by his old nature.

This statement reinforces the fact that there are two realms, the realm of the Spirit and the realm of the Law and never the twain shall meet. The believer is to choose from which realm he will operate. If he chooses to be led by the Spirit, he is not under the Law. The choice of one realm over the other will have consequences.

GALATIANS 5:19–21

*Now **the deeds of the flesh** are evident, which are: **immorality**, **impurity**, **sensuality**, ²⁰ **idolatry**, **sorcery**, **enmities**, **strife**, **jealousy**, **outbursts of anger**, **disputes**, **dissensions**, **factions**, ²¹ **envying**, **drunkenness**, **carousing**, and things like these, of which I forewarn you, just as I have forewarned you, that those who practice such things **will not inherit the kingdom of God**.*

The Deeds of the Flesh

Paul is specific about the results that accrue to a believer who lives in the realm of the flesh. Is it possible for a born again Christian to live such a life? The Bible reveals many real-life examples and specific statements by which the believer would say that the answer is "Yes!" with emphatic emphasis.

First Corinthians 3:1: "And I, brethren, could not speak to you as to spiritual men, but as to men of flesh, as to infants in Christ." The addressees are "brethren," a clear reference to their being believers. Then, a mere twelve words later, he calls them "men of flesh," repeating the fact that they are believers by calling them "infants in Christ."

In 1 Corinthians, "flesh" is *sarkinois*, an adjective. In Galatians 5:19, the believer has *sarkos*, the noun form of the same word. The same word in both texts shows that a believer can commit the sins of the flesh. In Galatians 5:13, Paul commands the "brethren" not to turn their freedom into an opportunity for the flesh. If the believer cannot walk according to the flesh, there would be no need for such an admonition. In Galatians 5:16, Paul tells the Galatians that if they walk by means of the Spirit, they will not carry out the desire of the flesh. It is therefore evident that the possibility exists that they may choose to walk by means of the flesh. In Galatians 6:8, the author warns his readers not to "sow to his own flesh, lest he harvest corruption.

158

The Scriptures contain accounts of believers who chose to be under the control of the flesh. Lot, the believer, (2 Pet 2:7) reaped a bitter harvest and Samson springs to mind as does Saul who tried to murder David and spent his last hours consulting the occult.

Even the greatest king of them all, David, harvested a whirlwind, committing adultery, getting a man drunk, then giving sealed orders that resulted in the killing of that same man. The doctrine of the existence of the sin nature is the easiest to prove; as Paul says, its "deeds are evident," which he emphasizes by putting "evident" first in the Greek text. In verses 19b–21, Paul begins a list of the works of the flesh.

Immorality

"Immorality" (*porneia*) is a general word for illegitimate sexual intercourse of all types. One refers to "traditional values," but the values called "traditional" are not at all traditional. The Christian ethic was on a collision course with traditional values in the Roman Empire. Matthew Rueger, in *Sexual Morality in a Christless World*, writes,

> He [the Roman male] would have sex with his slaves whether they were male or female; he would visit prostitutes; he would have homosexual encounters even while married; he would engage in pederasty; even rape was generally acceptable as long as he only raped people of a lower status.... "The first Christians were men and women of great courage.... Confessing Christian morality always requires that spirit of bravery.[101]

The discovery of the ancient cities of Pompe II and Herculaneum, both destroyed by Mt. Vesuvius in AD 79, revealed the cities to be rich in erotic artifacts such as statues, frescoes, and household items decorated with sexual themes. Such imagery was

---

[101] Quoted in "Three Awful Features of Roman Sexual Morality," https://www.challies.com/articles/3–awful-features-of-roman-sexual-morality/

everywhere and items indicate that the treatment of sexuality in ancient Rome was more relaxed than in Western culture influenced by Christianity.

First Corinthians shows how the new gentile converts to Christianity would have a lenient view of *porneia* and needed, not a minor realignment, but a major transformation.

Impurity

The word implies a *modus vivendi* that is utterly and shamelessly immoral (*akatharsia*). Isaiah writes a description of being shamelessly immoral: "The expression of their faces [the people of Jerusalem] bears witness against them, And they display their sin like Sodom; They do not *even* conceal *it*" (Isa 3:9). Far from concealing impurity, they flout it, delighting in it with in-your-face- celebrations. When a person reveals that he is a homosexual, the television audience applauds. Isaiah 5:20 speaks to the point: "Woe to those who call evil good, and good evil; Who substitute darkness for light and light for darkness; Who substitute bitter for sweet and sweet for bitter!" A T-shirt defiantly bore the words, "Homosexuality is not shameful, homophobia is."

Sensuality

This word (*aselgeia*) comes from a Persian city named Selge, a city known for its citizens who excelled in moral strictness. By attaching "a" (the alpha privative) to the word, the meaning is negated, resulting in the definition, "wanton (acts or) manners, as filthy words, indecent bodily movements."

Verse 20

Idolatry

The realm of the flesh engages in and promotes idolatry. The word literally means "image-worship" (*eidólolatria*). Each god needed an image—a statue or relief in stone or bronze—and an altar or temple at which to offer prayers and sacrifices. There were small images in the households of the heathen.

Sorcery

Occult practices were common in Asia Minor. There was a body of literature on the subject as seen in Acts 19:19. Portions of that literature survive. "Some of the magical texts found in Ephesus by archaeologists are now in the British Museum."[102]

For the people, there were incantations and spells.

Ancient Rome was a civilization defined by religious customs and magical practices. Magic spells were a significant part of ancient Roman culture; in fact, it is estimated that up to 80 percent of the population regularly used magic in some form or another. Magic was used in everyday life by ordinary people, including slaves, wealthy nobles and members of the court. It was also used for healing and for protection of both people and their possessions.[103]

Enmities, Strife, Jealousy, Outbursts of Anger, Disputes, Dissensions, Factions

Paul's list now turns to personal and social relationships. The first on the list is *echthra*, "hostilities, hatreds." This work of the flesh is in direct opposition to Christ's Upper Room discourse: "A new commandment I give to you, that you love one another, even as I have loved you, that you also love one another" (John 13:34). The disciples had seen the quality of His love for them ever since He called them. John recorded the most recent example of that

---

[102] Joseph P. Free, *Archaeology and Bible History*, 6th ed. (Wheaton: Scripture Press, 1959), 324.

[103] Moshe Rideout, "Ancient Rome," What Were Magic Spells in Ancient Rome?" https://www.learnancientrome.com/what-were-magic-spells-in-ancient-rome/

supernatural love in John 13, when He washed their feet, something they would not do for each other.

The watching world is not impressed when *echthra* arrives in the churches. *Echthra* diffuses tension throughout the body of Christ, a tension that affects the worship services, the "fellowship" dinners, even the congregational singing, *et al.*

The list sounds like it could be the honest minutes of a church business meeting controlled by *Robert's Rules of Order* instead of the Holy Spirit. If 2 Peter 1:3 is true, why is it necessary to import *Robert's Rules of Order* into the meetings?

Regarding every business meeting, there is an unnoticed elephant in the room: democracy. It is democracy, in league with the flesh, that produces the chaos of Paul's list: strife, factions, outbursts of temper, anger, disputes, and dissensions.

This may sound un-American, but the Founding Fathers rejected democracy. As Steve Hanke points out: At the founding of America,

> Neither the President, members of the judiciary nor the Senate were elected directly by a vote of the people. Only the members of the House of Representatives were directly elected by popular vote. Many will be shocked to learn that the word 'democracy' was neither used in the Declaration of Independence nor in the Constitution. Indeed, the Founding Fathers were anxious and fearful of allowing any form of tyranny, including the tyranny of the majority.[104]

On various issues to come before the church, factions form, clandestine meetings are held, and non-members are encouraged by each faction to join the church so they can vote the "right" way.

---

[104] Steve Hanke, Cato Institute, "On Democracy Versus Liberty," January 20, 2011. https://www.cato.org/commentary/democracy-versus-liberty#

Once the issue is voted "yea or nay," new factions form for the next meeting.

In a letter from John Adams to whom John Adams wrote, "Remember Democracy never lasts long. It soon wastes, exhausts and murders itself. There never was a Democracy Yet, that did not commit suicide."[105] The church is founded on the Word of God, not the parliamentary procedures of the American House of Representatives.

Verse 21

Envying, Drunkenness, Carousing

Paul completes his list of personal relationships with "envyings" (*phthonos*), a word connoting "grudges" accompanied by "the miserable trait of being glad when someone experiences misfortune or pain."[106] When the meeting is over, spiritual scar tissue remains in the form of soul-grinding grudges and ill wills that will not soon be forgotten.

Paul now moves to works of the flesh dealing with self-control, starting with "intoxication" (*methé*). Paul connects this excess with "carousings," (*kómos*). *Kómos* in the Greek culture referred to "a nocturnal and riotous procession of half-drunken and frolicsome fellows who after supper parade through the streets with torches and music in honor of Bacchus or some other deity and sing and play before the houses of their male and female friends."[107] These were drinking parties that went until the early hours of the morning.

In the Roman Empire Bacchus, the god of wine and revelry, had his own cult. The Romans were afraid of this god. "Bacchus

---

[105] Reproduced in its original form.

[106] Thayer, 652.

[107] Thayer, 395.

and his cult earned a reputation for dangerous excess. The immorality and debauchery of their rituals were so shocking that some of Rome's greatest writers decried the cult as a threat to the state."[108]

There is abundant ancient testimony that portrays the Galatians as being especially prone to these excesses. These vices were a feature of the Galatian character, which Peter mentions in 1 Peter 4:3. In cultures, ancient and modern, an intoxicated person has been portrayed as entertaining and comedic, but the truth is, there is nothing funny about a drunk.

Those Will Not Inherit the Kingdom

During Paul's time with the Galatians, his teaching ministry involved warning them against the results of walking in the realm of the flesh, thereby showing that those who say a true Christian could not commit the list of the above sins are naive.

His teaching consisted of warning them that "while all will enter the Messianic kingdom, not all will inherit the Messianic kingdom, meaning not all will be rewarded and have a position of honor and glory in the kingdom...if they are true believers, they will be dealt with by God in such a way that they will either repent or they will be taken by divine discipline to Heaven early."

With that specific list, Paul contrasts the results of walking by means of the Holy Spirit as over and against walking in the realm of the flesh. The contrast is dramatic.

---

[108] Mike Greenberg, *Mythology Source,* "Bacchus: The Roman God of Wine," January 4, 2021, https://shorturl.at/okZ4c.

GALATIANS 5:22–26

*But **the fruit of the Spirit** is love, joy, peace, patience, kindness, goodness, faithfulness, [23] gentleness, self-control; **against such things there is no law**. [24] Now those who belong to Christ Jesus have **crucified the flesh** with its passions and desires. [25] **If we live by the Spirit**, let us also **walk by the Spirit**. [26] Let us not become **boastful**, **challenging** one another, **envying** one another.*

Verse 22–23

The Fruit of the Spirit

These two verses have been called the shortest biography of Christ ever written. These verses render the evidence of walking in the realm of the Spirit. It is to be noticed that whereas the results of walking by means of the flesh produce chaos in the life of the believer and in the church, the fruit of the Spirit produces the opposite.

The word picture of "fruit" is an apt one. Fruit have been a recurring theme in still-life paintings throughout history because of its visual appeal. They provide a variety of colors and textures for artists to explore. Their vibrant hues and diverse shapes make them captivating subjects in still-life compositions.

In Proverbs 25:11, the author made this comparison, "Like apples of gold in settings of silver is a word spoken in right circumstances." Satan used the beauty of fruit in the temptation and fall of man: "When the woman saw that the tree was…a delight to the eyes…she took from its fruit and ate (Genesis 3:6).

Paul uses the singular, "fruit," not "fruits." The Spirit produces these virtues as a unity which means that if one of the virtues is missing, then the believer does not have the fruit of the Spirit.

165

This fruit has nine flavors in the form of various virtues which can be grouped: "Love, joy, peace" are inward; "Patience, kindness, goodness" are outward; Faithfulness, gentleness, self-control" are upward. "Gentleness" (*prautés*) connotes humility in one's life. A humble person will make others a success at his expense.

No Law Against Such Things

The Law could never produce this fruit. The results of a life lived in the realm of the Spirit is a life on a higher plane than the Law, and the law of Moses can find no flaw in the fruit of the Spirit.

When one thinks of the contrast of the realm of the flesh and the realm of the Holy Spirit, "There are laws in society against the deeds of the flesh because they are destructive, but there are none against the fruit of the Spirit, because it is edifying. The works of the flesh know no law, but the fruit of the Spirit needs no law. This fruit involves both character and conduct."[109]

Verse 24

The Crucified Flesh

Experientially, the sin nature remains a constant nagging companion of the believer, however, when of the believer's salvation, he now stands on new ground positionally in Christ. Positionally, the believer has become a new creation in Christ Jesus as 2 Corinthians 5:17 reveals: "Therefore if anyone is in Christ, he is a new creature; the old things passed away; behold, new things have come." His old position in Adam is gone. As Paul writes, "For as in Adam all die, so also in Christ all will be made alive" (1 Cor 15:22).

---

[109] James E. Rosscup, "Fruit in the New Testament," *Bibliotheca Sacra* 125:497 (January-March 1968): 56–66.

Since the flesh has been dealt a lethal blow, the believer, experientially, is no longer under its control unless he chooses to be. This initiates a struggle between the flesh and the Spirit. The unbeliever has no choice; he has no power to walk by means of the Spirit. The believer has a choice and can choose to produce the beautiful fruit of the Spirit. The admonition for the believer is to live in consistency with his position.

In Galatians 5:25–6:10, Paul begins a section in which he records the principles of daily living in society. He begins with a military analogy.

Verse 25

If We Live by the Spirit

"If" begins this section and it's a first-class condition which means, "if, and it's true," which, in this context means that it's true that the believer has a new life, and "life" implies activity. Living does not imply passivity; the believer is to do something with his life. To show what one should do with this new life, Paul turns to his knowledge of military life.

Walk by the Spirit

Paul often saw and came into contact up close and personal with the Roman military. He had seen the greatest army of his day marching through the streets. When he wrote the word "walk," he was visualizing the soldiers "marching in rank" (*stoicheó*), precisely in step, each with the other. This is what he's communicating and commanding in this verse: "Keep in step with the Spirit."

It would be an awkward sight to see just one soldier marching out of step with others. It would not only be awkward but also disruptive to the progress of the platoon. This makes Paul's choice of this word exactly the precise word because, from this point until 6:10, he will examine the subject of the daily social activities with his fellow "soldiers" and with those not in the platoon.

167

Verse 26

Boasting

In keeping with the motif of marching in rank with the Holy Spirit and others, Paul shows examples of what to do and what to avoid so as to march in rank—the believer, to stay in step, is not to become "conceited" (*kenodoxos*). This Greek word is a combination of two: *kenos*, "empty" and *doxa*, "glory," thus, "empty glory."

Conceit is often subtle. One way is with the humblebrag, which is a person's attempt to impress others while trying to look humble: "I don't know why people say I'm such a good speaker," Or, "Don't you just hate it when you go somewhere, and they can't break a $100 bill for you?" Or, a parent says, "I can't believe I spilled water all over the papers I need to sign to put Dylan in the gifted program."

Challenging

This word (*prokaleó*) has to do with deliberately irritating someone. When coupled with the characteristic of conceit, the conceited believer is a believer who enjoys being an irritant to others and therefore, is out of step with his platoon.

Envying

The last in the list is *phthonos*, meaning "envy/jealousy" Envy is the "green-eyed monster." This expression goes back to Shakespeare who employed the word picture. In *Othello*, where Iago says, "O, beware, my lord, of jealousy; It is the green-eyed monster which doth mock the meat it feeds on."[110]

Green has long been a color associated with sickness, because people's skin sometimes can take on a slightly

---

[110] Shakespeare, *Othello*, Act 3, Scene 3.

yellow/green tinge when they are seriously ill. Jealousy/envy operate like a morally debilitating sickness.

This "monster" can be subtle as well. It occurs when you tell an impressive story but there's that one in the group that feels he must render an account that tops your story. He must be center stage.

GALATIANS 6:1–5

*Brethren, even if anyone is **caught in any trespass**, **you who are spiritual**, **restore** such a one in a **spirit of gentleness**; each one looking to yourself, so that you too **will not be tempted**. [2] **Bear one another's burdens**, and thereby **fulfill the law of Christ**. [3] For if anyone **thinks he is something** when he is nothing, he deceives himself. [4] But **each one must examine his own work**, and then he will have reason for **boasting in regard to himself alone**, and not in regard to another. [5] **For each one will bear his own load.***

Caught in Trespass

In another of those texts which prove that believers can walk according to the flesh, a Christian can be "caught in a trespass." "Caught" (*prolambanó*) refers to cases of surprise, or of sudden temptation…they may be surprised by sudden temptation, or urged on by impetuous or headstrong passion, as Peter's denial of knowing Jesus was.[111]

The verb indicates the trespass was not a willful sin with malice aforethought. The sinner in such a case was not vigilant and was not guarding his soul.

You who are Spiritual

Such a believer caught in a trespass is operating in the realm of the flesh and has broken ranks. He needs a ministry of reconciliation. This ministry is not open to every believer; those who are spiritual are to engage in the process. The classic Old Testament example of "you who are spiritual" is the prophet Nathan who skillfully confronted David (2 Sam 12). This is not a

---

[111]Barnes' Notes on the Bible, Gal. 6:1.

ministry for new believers, those who are immature, or those believers who are carnal.

Those who are spiritual are those in the body of Christ, the mature believers who have a record of consistency (not perfection which is impossible), of marching in step with others and the Spirit, and giving evidence of the fruit of the Spirit.

This text shows that not all the Galatians have deserted the grace system; there are those who are in step with the Spirit within the churches.

Restore

"Restore" (*katartizó*) describes a necessary activity of fishermen with their nets as in Mark 1:19: "Going on a little farther, He saw James the son of Zebedee, and John his brother, who were also in the boat mending the nets." The word describes the skill and care seen in a fisherman restoring his nets to their former functioning capacity.

The restoration process is not punitive. In the context, the goal would be helping the individual get back in the marching ranks. This is where 1 John 1:9 would come into play by his recognizing and confessing the sin, that is, "agreeing" (*homologeó* "to say the same thing") with God that he has broken ranks.

A Spirit of Gentleness

Paul moves to describe how those who are spiritual are to operate: without arrogance, impatience, or anger. They are not to think in terms of making their brother pay, in the spirit of revenge as they take their pound of flesh. Gentleness would eliminate an attitude of condemnation. Those who are spiritual would be the opposite of the domineering and arrogant Diotrephes recorded in 2 John 9–10.

Will Not Be Tempted

Those who are spiritual will have the attitude of "There but for the grace of God go I." The Bible is clear in its warnings, "Take heed, lest you fall" (1 Cor 10:12). Temptations abound. There is the saying, "The flesh is weak." How often has it been said with a conceited and smug arrogance, "I'll never do that!" and it becomes the very thing done when in the pressure cooker of temptation.

The classic example of this is found in Matthew 26:33: "But Peter said to Him, 'Even though all may fall away because of You, I will never fall away.'" The Greek text is emphatic: "I will never, not even one time, fall away!" Second Samuel 1:19 can be written over Peter's under-pressure conduct at that infamous campfire: "How have the mighty fallen!"

Verse 2

Bear One Another's Burdens

Another aspect of marching together destroys a popular Christian myth. Regarding the word, "burdens" (*baros*), it is "a load of an excessive weight, such as it is a toil to carry."[112]

Well-meaning but misinformed people often repeat the never-dying fantasy, "God never gives you more than you can handle," not realizing the dominoes that fall from such a belief. The major problem with this bromide is that, if it's true, then there is no need of God; the believer is self-sufficient. Another problem is, if that statement is true, then why would Paul include this verse in the epistle? This command is a call to lend a helping hand and to pray for the overwhelmed brother, whether he's being overwhelmed by sin or finances, or other circumstances.

---

[112] The Pulpit Commentary, https://biblehub.com/commentaries/galatians/6–2.htm.

Fulfill the Law of Christ

This text recognizes that the believer, though not under the Mosaic law, is under law—the law of Christ. This means that when the Christian steals or commits adultery, for example, he's not breaking the Mosaic law; he's not under the Law given on Mt. Sinai. He's breaking the law of Christ.

Some of the laws of the Mosaic code are carried over into the law of Christ. It is still a sin to commit murder, to covet, and to steal in the Dispensation of the Church, for example. Looking at it another way, England has some laws that are like laws in America but that does not mean that Americans are under British law.

This surfaces the question, what is the law of Christ that the believer is to fulfill? The law of Christ encompasses the commands Jesus gave in the Upper Room Discourse such as John 13:34, 14:15. The law of Christ would include the commands in the epistles and Revelation 1–3.

Verse 3

Thinks He is Something

In these verses, at first glance, Paul appears to be contradicting himself because he's just instructed, "Bear one another's burdens." Now he is saying, "each one must bear his own load."

A close examination proves there's no contradiction. The believer who thinks himself to be above others (conceited), is placing himself above helping others and instead of serving, he deems himself to be one to be served. In that upper room, no disciple filled a basin of water, took a towel, and began to wash eleven pairs of dirty feet. Each one believed himself to be better than doing a slave's menial and dirty task.

Such a person's conceit is delusional, a person living in a fantasy world. The worst part of it all is that he has deluded

173

himself to believe, like the emperor in the Hans Christian Anderson fairy tale, that he's wearing a fine set of clothes when he's parading before one and all in his underwear. Such a person is not marching in the ranks.

Verse 4

Each Must Examine His Own Work

An "examination" ("scrutinize," *dokimazo*) would remind the believer that no one in himself is superior to another. An objective review of one's accomplishments should also bring to memory that the only legitimate ground for justifiable self-satisfaction is God's enablement.

Boasting in Regard to Himself Alone

In context, Paul is admonishing the believer not to think highly of himself because of his contrasting himself with others. There is an outrageous example of just such boasting in Luke 18:9–12, a text in which a self-satisfied and insufferable Pharisee congratulates himself for "not [being] like other people."

But the Pharisee did not stop there: he becomes specific in his *bragamony* by comparing himself with robbers, adulterers et al. If a believer is going to boast, let him compare himself with the word of God, with the law of Christ, not the real or supposed shortcomings of others, he alone with his Bible should scrutinize himself.

Verse 5

Each One will Bear His Own Load

This brings the reader to a supposed contradiction in the epistle. One the one hand, Paul says to "bear one another's burdens" (v. 2), then on the other hand, he commands that "each one will bear his own load" (v. 5). The "problem" is easily resolved by noticing that the translators, to clarify what Paul is writing, use two English words: in verse 2, he writes "burdens;" in verse 5, he writes "load." The reason for this translation is that he uses two separate Greek words which the NASB reflects by using two different English words.

In verse 2, "burden" is *baros*, a heavy weight a person is unable to carry without assistance, while in verse 5, the word is *phortion*, the Greek word for a workload that anyone can carry by himself with no assistance. By understanding that there is no contradiction, there is an example of what to do when confronted with Bible critics who say they have found contradictions: dig deeper. Do not be satisfied and take the critic's evaluation as legitimate.

Paul is saying that each believer has his own personal responsibilities and is accountable to God to take care of them (e.g., 1 Tim 5:8).

GALATIANS 6:6–10

The One who is Taught the Word is to Share All Good Things with the One who Teaches Him. [7] *Do not be* **deceived***: God is not be* **mocked***. A man reaps what he sows.* [8] *Whoever sows to please their flesh, from the flesh will reap* **destruction;** *whoever sows to please the Spirit, from the Spirit will reap* **eternal life.** [9] *Let us not* **lose heart** *in doing good, for in due time* **we will reap** *if we do not* **grow weary***. So then, while we have opportunity, let us* **do good to all people***, and especially to* **those who are of the household of the faith***.*

Verse 6

There needs to be an exclamation point after this verse; it is neglected. The careful reader will notice the place this command occupies: it is after "bearing one another's burdens." Therefore, in context, this sharing is a way to obey that command.

This command is part of the law of Christ: if a person is benefiting spiritually from the instruction of a teacher of the Word, he has an obligation to share his material goods with that teacher. Paul speaks to this point in 1 Timothy 5:18: "For the Scripture says, 'You shall not muzzle the ox while he is threshing,' and 'The laborer is worthy of his wages.'"

The modern reader reads (and maybe heeds) this command with tunnel vision. He understands the text to say, "…to share with the pastor all good things." The problem is that the verse is not limited to one's pastor. The Bible-teaching pastor is included but this verse is not about an army of one; it's more general than that. This text would encompass Sunday school teachers, home Bible class teachers, radio ministries, authors, those from whom a person is learning the Scriptures.

A sad situation developed in a local church concerning the daughters of the pastor who were regular attenders of the youth

176

group. The group held a social outing at a skating rink. The attendance was a good one with the kids enjoying showing off their skills on the rink, that is, all but two laced up their roller skates that night—the pastor's daughters.

The reason they were not on the rink was because the family did not have enough money for the girls' night of fun with the group. Whether such a disregard of Galatians 6:6 affected the girls later in life is unknown, but it must have hurt for a long time afterward.

The one taught might share to help with a car repair or a medical expense. There are various ways to "share."

A man was applying to be the pastor of a church, and when it came time to discuss financial arrangements, the chairman of the board informed him that, when he became the pastor, in addition to his salary, "Farmer Jones will bring you a turkey every once in a while." When the church did select him as their new pastor, he said, "Thanks, but no thanks," knowing that his support would be meager to the point of a turkey here and there.

Verses 7

Deceived

The conceited believer who does not share with those instructing him is deceiving himself to think that he's in step with the Spirit. To keep in step, the believer must plan properly, and when he does, a proper harvest will come. In the context, the previous verse delineated the principle of a believer who is being instructed in the word is to share what he has with the one teaching him the word.

It is within that context that Paul issues a sudden warning: if a person is self-centered and does not share what he has, God will not multiply what he has and bless him.

If he is out of step and follows the inclination of the flesh, he will reap death ("destruction"), but if he follows the Spirit ("sows to the Spirit") he will reap eternal life.

Mocked

When a believer refuses to share with the one(s) instructing him in the truth, it is a serious matter as reflected in the word "mocked" (*muktérizó*). Paul employs a word picture of rebellion, "to turn up the nose at someone." Paul describes persistently refusing to sow in accord with the leading of the Holy Spirit as sneering at God.

Verse 8

Destruction & Eternal Life

"Destruction" carries the concept of "decay," "ruin." (*phthoran*). His meager harvest will not be what it could have been. The words of John Greenleaf Whittier would apply in this case: "For all sad words of tongue and pen, The saddest are these, 'It might have been.'"[113]

In contrast, the harvest of the believer marching in the ranks to the will of the Spirit will be that of eternal life. It's important to note that the Bible uses "eternal life" in two senses. "On the one hand, the New Testament writers spoke of it as a gift that one receives by faith (John 10:28; *et al.*). However, eternal life also refers to the quality of the believer's life, which depends on the extent to which he or she walks with God in fellowship (John 10:10). In this second sense some believers experience eternal life to a greater degree than other believers do. It is in this second sense that Paul spoke of eternal life [in Gal 6:8].[114]

---

[113] John Greenleaf Whittier, "Maud Muller."

[114] See Dillow, 135–45; Zane C. Hodges, *The Gospel Under Siege*, 81; and Robert N. Wilkin, "Sow for It! Reaping Abundant Eternal Life

Verse 9

Paul has now come to the last of the evidence to recognize one's marching in the ranks with the Spirit and with others.

Lose Heart

Even though there is a verse division at the point, one should not lose sight of the sowing/reaping word picture. From the ancient and the modern viewpoint, raising crops is wearisome, back-breaking labor. The searing sun, the constant care, the sometimes-necessary protection from a coming plunge in temperatures, can wear and tear body and soul. Perhaps Paul had seen a farmer faint or grow weak in the heat. The analogy is an apt one. Paul knew about toil and trouble in the work as in 2 Corinthians 11 where he details the hardships he faced.

"Lose heart" (*ekkakeó*) speaks of being "without spirit," "exhausted" and thus becoming faint-hearted. Paul calls for perseverance in the work.

We will Reap

The God who cannot lie makes the sowing believer in step with the Spirit an encouraging promise: "You will reap!" There will be a time of the harvesting. That time is in God's hands; some of the harvest may be in this life but if not, the harvest will come at the Bema Seat of Christ when the believer's harvest is shown to be gold, silver, and precious stones.

Grow Weary

The great harvest will come for the believer who does not "grow weary" (*eklyomenoi*) and therein lies a word picture of an archer relaxing the bowstring, a picture of giving up.

---

as a Reward (Galatians 6:8–9)," *Grace Evangelical Society News* 5:8 (August 1990): 2.

A study of church history is a study of the many giants of the faith who did not loosen the bowstring. Adoniram and his wife Ann Judson serve as a premiere example.

When the couple arrived in Burma, he and Ann learned the language. It took him years to do it, but he translated the entire Bible into Burmese. Although they told the people about Jesus all the time, it took six years (!) before one person accepted Jesus as his Savior.

Adoniram and Ann went through many hard times in Burma. The poor food, unbearable heat, and widespread diseases made life difficult. Two of their babies died in the terrible climate, and both Ann and Adoniram were imprisoned during the war with Britain.

But when Adoniram Judson died in 1850, there were 7,000 baptized believers, 63 Christian congregations and 163 missionaries in Burma. To this day, over 150 years later, his Burmese Bible translation is still in use.[115]

That is a remarkable harvest!

Verse 10

Do Good to All People

The in-step believer will do what is "morally good" (*agathos*), literally, "to all." The operative word is "morally." The drug addict might think the good thing to do for him is to enable him to get his next dose of heroin which would not be the moral thing to do.

---

[115] From "Christianity.com,
https://www.christianity.com/church/church-history/church-history-for-kids/adoniram-judson-first-missionary-from-the-united-states-1163504
4.html.

A believer wanted to do good to his neighbors and decided to shovel snow off their sidewalks and driveways. He physically could not do all those areas on his block, but he could do some as he had the opportunity and strength.

Those of the Household of Faith

Paul points out that there is a hierarchy in doing good to all. At times, there arises the need for a choice, that is, to do good for the unsaved or to do good to the household of faith. To use the earlier analogy, the man would shovel the snow from his family's driveway and sidewalks first. In reference to the household of faith, it is, "spiritual family first."

> Every poor and distressed man had [sic] a claim on me for pity, and, if I can afford it, for active exertion and pecuniary relief. But a poor Christian has a far stronger claim on my feelings, my labors, and my property. He is my brother, equally interested as myself in the blood and love of the Redeemer. I expect to spend an eternity with him in heaven. He is the representative of my unseen Savior, and he considers everything done to his poor afflicted as done to himself. For a Christian to be unkind to a Christian is not only wrong, it is monstrous.[116]

---

[116] Ronald Y. K. Fung, *The Epistle to the Galatians*, New International Commentary on the New Testament series (Grand Rapids: Wm. B. Eerdmans Publishing Co., 1988), 275.

THE CONCLUSION

GALATIANS 6:11-18

GALATIANS 6:11–13

*See with **what large letters I am writing to you with my own hand**. [12] Those who desire **to make a good showing** in the flesh try to compel you to be circumcised, simply so that they will **not be persecuted for the cross of Christ**. [13] For those who are circumcised **do not even keep the Law themselves**, but they desire to have you circumcised so that they may boast in your flesh.*

Verse 11

Large Letters by My Own Hand

Paul's sign-off presents two options: he takes the quill and scroll from his secretary to whom he's been dictating the epistle and writes this verse, or he's written the entire epistle and now draws attention to the large letters, which may be a reference to the aforementioned problem with his eyes. Whatever option one takes, Paul is focusing the attention of the Galatians on his concluding remarks. Paul turns the readers' focus on the Judaizers and warns them about three of their characteristics.

Verse 12

First, they want to brag about the number of their Gentile converts. They want this number to look good on their reports back to headquarters. "To make a good showing" (*euprosopeo*) incorporates the idea of "to make a display, "to make a good show." Their desire is in the realm of the flesh. Paul's words bring to mind his former membership in the group to whom Christ said, "Woe to you, scribes and Pharisees, hypocrites, because you travel around on sea and land to make one proselyte..." (Matt 23:15).

Secondly, Paul cites another aspect of their motivation: so that they will not be persecuted for the cross of Christ. Legalism persecutes grace as illustrated in Paul's allegory of the

184

Ishmael/Isaac on-going conflict. The religions of the world with their works do not raise the fury from the world but the declaration of the finished work of Christ does. To combine law and grace would be the way to avoid persecution because the world loves a world system for salvation. The Judaizers could hide under the cover of Judaism if the prying eyes of Rome came around.

Verse 13

In the third place, the legalists are inconsistent. They do not even keep the Law themselves. Jesus pointed to their blatant hypocrisy in Mark 12 when He brought their attention to the fact that under the Law, the Jews were to care for and protect the widows, when, truth be told, the scribes and Pharisees "devour widows' houses."[117]

In Jesus' fiery denunciation of religion in Matthew 23:2–4, He said, "The scribes and the Pharisees have seated themselves in the chair of Moses; therefore, all that they tell you, do and observe, but do not do according to their deeds; for they say *things* and do not do *them*. They tie up heavy burdens and lay them on men's shoulders, but they themselves are unwilling to move them with *so much as* a finger."

The hypocrisy continues to this day in the form of a lordship salvationist's gospel invitation telling people that to be saved, they must abandon their sins, something they themselves have not done (1 John 1:8).

---

[117] cf. Deut 24:17, 19–21; 26:12, *et al.*

GALATIANS 6:14–16

*But may it never be that I would **boast**, except **in the cross** of our Lord Jesus Christ, through which **the world has been crucified to me, and I to the world.*** *[15] For **neither** is **circumcision** anything, **nor uncircumcision**, but **a new creation.** [16] And those who will **walk by this rule**, peace and mercy be upon them, and upon the Israel of God.*

Verse 14

Boast in the Cross

Literally, the verse begins with, "For me" (*emoi*), which Paul places first places for emphasis to show the difference between Paul and the Judaizers.

In contrast to the motivation of the false teachers, Paul records the *raison d'être* for his ministry: "to rejoice, to glory in" (*kauchaomai*) the cross.

This statement by Paul has lost its shock value today. Two thousand years ago, crucifixion was such a shameful death that no Roman citizen could legally, suffer that most tortuous form of punishment and only rarely for certain crimes such as treason.

"In 70 BC the Roman orator Cicero prosecuted Verres, the Roman governor of Sicily, for malpractice and cruelty while in office. Cicero claimed that Verres had ordered a Roman citizen, Gavius, to be stripped and beaten and then crucified.[118] No one would wear a cross as a necklace or earrings in Paul's day.

---

[118] University of Cambridge School of Classics, "Rome In Focus," Roman law: the art of the fair and good? The protection of citizenship, 186

The World Crucified

The world-system (*kosmos*) is organized to leave God out and has an attractive glamour (cf. Matt 4:8). For Paul, that glamor has no magnetism; he's dead to it. But for a countless number, the world-system has an omnipotent pull.

A world-famous actor revealed in his memoir that, as a young teen, he got on his knees, closed his eyes, and prayed: "God, you can do whatever you want to me, just please make me famous."

In a classic case of being careful what you pray for, he became famous, exceedingly so. By the time he was 18, he had developed a habit of drinking every day, yet he thought that becoming a famous star in Hollywood would help cure his addiction. However, the fame of being a celebrity worsened his addiction.

At age 54, he was found floating face down in the pool of his Pacific Palisades home. He was unconscious in a stand-alone jacuzzi. He was reported to be receiving ketamine infusion therapy for depression and anxiety.

Ketamine has medical and surgical uses as an anesthetic and is also known as a recreational drug mainly due to its dissociative nature, indicating disconnection of mind and body. It can also have short duration hallucinatory and psychedelic effects. It was on that, he overdosed. The Sirens' song of *kosmos* glamor inexorably drew him to his death.

Verse 15

Neither Circumcision nor Uncircumcision

Once more, with feeling, Paul pounds the final nail into place. Regarding a person's right standing before God, both

---

https://www.romansinfocus.com/sites/www.romansinfocus.com/files/Protection%20of%20citizenship.pdf

circumcision and uncircumcision are worthless; they mean nothing. Yet, the wolves had been making it to be of first importance. (contra 1 Cor 15:3)

To gain a balanced picture: circumcision is important for the Jews as a sign of the Abrahamic covenant, being necessary for their obedience, just as baptism is important for the follower of Christ as an act of obedience. But neither count toward justification (cf. 1 Cor 1:17).

A New Creation

A right standing before God has one and only one condition: belief, and that belief produces regeneration through the cross of Christ. At that point, the believer becomes a new creation positionally, the old position in Adam has passed away (2 Cor 5:17).

Lewis Sperry Chafer, reflecting on the believer's position in Christ, wrote of the "Thirty-Three Riches of Divine Grace all of which come as a result of his position in Christ."[119]

Verse 16

Walk by This Rule

The "rule" (*kanón*) to which Paul refers furnishes the English language with the word "canon," meaning, "a rod or straight piece of rounded wood to which anything is fastened to keep it straight." The canon to which Paul refers is the seeing of the worthlessness of circumcision and uncircumcision regarding justification.

---

[119] Lewis Sperry Chafer, "The Riches Of Divine Grace: Thirty-Three Stupendous Works of God which Together Comprise the Salvation of An Individuals Soul," in Chafer Systematic Theology, vol. 3, *Soteriology* (Dallas Seminary Press: Dallas, TX, 1948), 234–66.

Paul says, "Peace and mercy be upon them and the Israel of God [who walk by the aforementioned rule]." The identity of the Israel of God has sparked debate.

The first question to answer is, "To whom does the word *them* refer?" This would be a reference to the believing gentiles in the Galatian churches, based upon the identity of "the Israel of God," who are separate from "them." The only possible answer is that, separate from the gentiles would be the Jews.

There are those who identify the Israel of God as the church. However, "From the standpoint of biblical usage this view stands condemned. There is no instance in biblical literature of the term *Israel* being used in the sense of the church, or the people of God as composed of both believing ethnic Jews and gentiles... thus the usage of the term *Israel* stands overwhelmingly opposed to [the view that the church is the Israel of God].[120]

"The church is never called 'spiritual Israel,' or 'a new Israel.' The term *Israel* is either used of the nation or the people as a whole, or of the believing Remnant within. It is never used of the church in general or of Gentile believers in particular."[121]

To transform the church into the New Israel is to spiritualize and thus rob Israel of its covenants and promises which fill the Old Testament.

---

[120] S. Lewis Johnson, "Paul and 'The Israel of God:' An Exegetical Case Study," The Master's Seminary Journal Spring 2009, 41–43.

[121] Fruchtenbaum, 66.

GALATIANS 6:17–18

*From now on **let no one cause trouble for me**, for I bear on my body **the brand-marks of Jesus Christ**. The grace of our Lord Jesus Christ be with your spirit, brethren. Amen.*

Let No One Cause Trouble for Me

The legalists have done to Paul what legalists do: they have caused him a great deal of trouble, (*kopos*), a word involving "intense labor united with trouble, toil." Paul puts "trouble" in the plural, "troubles." It has taken a toll upon him physically and spiritually as he's defended his gift and calling, his relationship to the apostles, the source of his gospel and teaching (Christ), and his vigorous apologetic for the one requirement for salvation: belief alone.

The Brand-Marks of Jesus

"Brand marks" is transliterated directly into English with the Greek word, *stigmata*. Paul borrowed the concept from 1st century culture: a *stigma* (singular) was

> a mark pricked in or branded upon the body. According to ancient oriental usage, slaves and soldiers bore the name or stamp of their master or commander branded or pricked (cut) into their bodies to indicate what master or general they belonged to, and there were even some devotees who stamped themselves in this way with the token of their gods.[122]

By this word, the apostle was showing that he belongs in every way to Jesus.

---

[122] Thayer, 588.

The brand-marks to which Paul refers are both physical and spiritual. Second Corinthians 11:22–28 bears witness to his *stigmata,* as would his stoning at Lystra and his beating at Philippi. These would leave visible, life-long scars. The scars Paul bore would contrast with the false teachers whose skin bore no ugly disfigurement.

As Paul bids an epistolary farewell, the reader is reminded of the strident words with which he began the letter. That tone is gone; the ending is soft, gentle, and compassionate. He ends with "the grace of our Lord Jesus Christ," and, finally as a poignant touch, "brethren, Amen."

SCRIPTURE INDEX

4:1	83
5:8	87
5:18	86
6:20	54

2 Timothy

1:14	54
3:12	8
3:12	68
3:16	34

Titus

1:6	93
1:10–11	73

Hebrews

7	64
12:2	8

James

1:25	57
2:10	76
3:1	73

1 Peter

1:2	66
4:3	73

2 Peter

2:1	50
2:2,	50
3:17	63

1 John 5:19   7

2 John

7	50
10–11	3, 42

Revelation

1:1–3	46
2:2	4
18:23	93
20:11	84
21:3	93

www.ingramcontent.com/pod-product-compliance
Lightning Source LLC
LaVergne TN
LVHW041316080426
835513LV00008B/488